VANESSA-ANN'S 101 CHRISTMAS ORNAMENTS

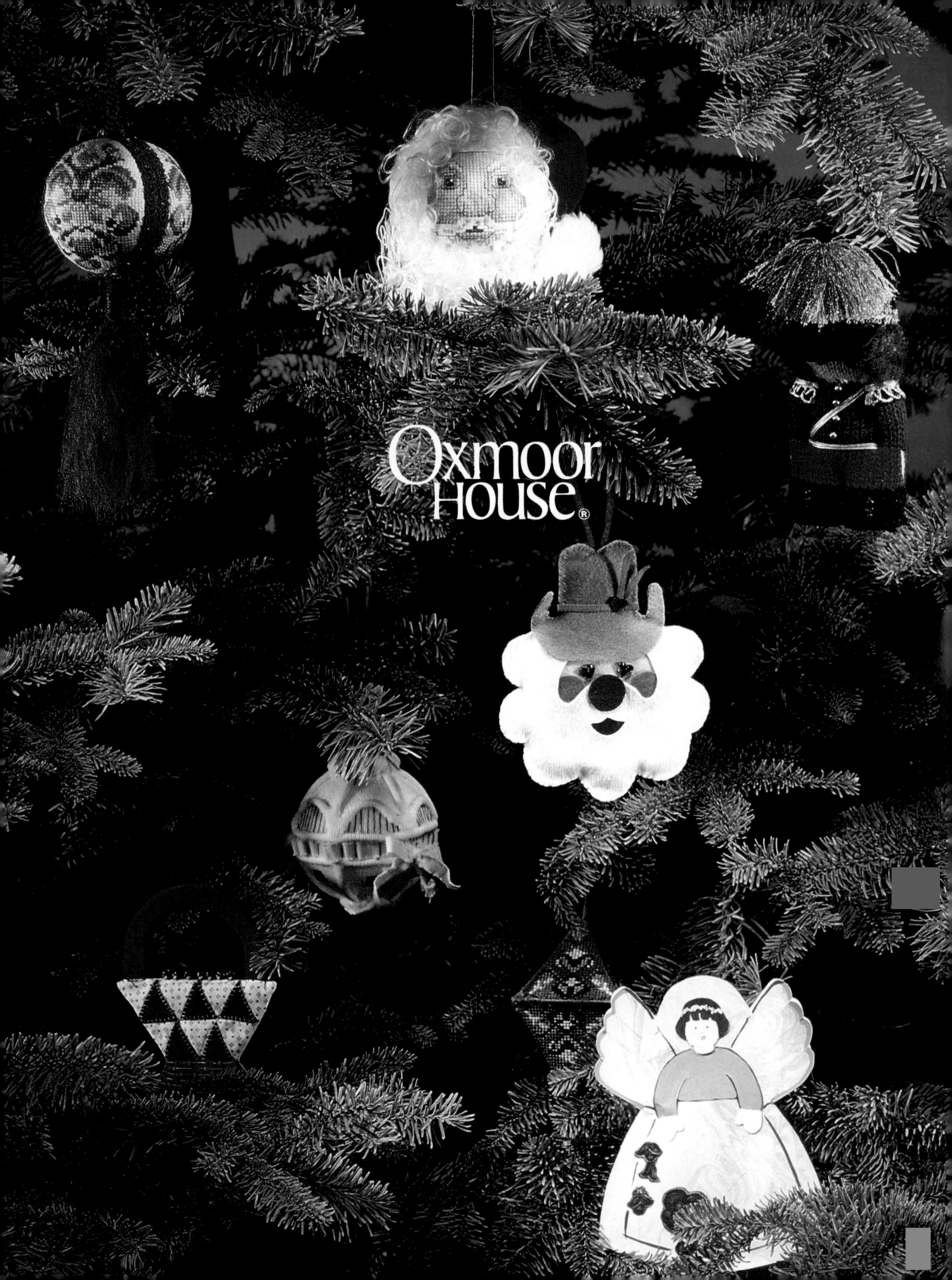
Oxmoor House®

To Nancy,
You have become our teacher, our confidant, and our friend.
You have helped us be what we had only imagined. Because
of everything you are and all you do, we have come both to
love and admire you.

Jo and Terrece

For The Vanessa-Ann Collection
Owners: Jo Packham and Terrece Beesley
Designers: Terrece Beesley, Trice Boerens, Kim Brown, Linda Durbano,
    Debbie Hardy, Meredith Johnson, Carol Krob, Marlene Lund, Jo Packham,
    Susan Pendleton, Florence Stacey
Staff: Ana Ayala, Gloria Zirkel Baur, Sandra Durbin Chapman, Holly Fuller,
    Susan Jorgensen, Margaret Shields Marti, Barbara Milburn, Lisa Miles,
    Pamela Randall, Lynda Sorenson, Florence Stacey, Nancy Whitley
Book Design: Baker Design Group
Photographer: Ryne Hazen

The Vanessa-Ann Collection wishes to thank Trends and Traditions in
Ogden, Utah, and Every Blooming Thing in Salt Lake City, Utah, for their
trust and cooperation with the photography of this book.

©1992 by Oxmoor House, Inc.
Book Division of Southern Progress Corporation
P.O. Box 2463, Birmingham, AL 35201

Library of Congress Catalog Number: 9260990
ISBN: 0-8487-1080-0
Manufactured in the United States of America
First Printing

Editor-in-Chief: Nancy Fitzpatrick
Director of Manufacturing: Jerry Higdon
Art Director: James Boone
Copy Chief: Mary Jean Haddin

Vanessa-Ann's 101 Christmas Ornaments
from the *Quick & Easy ScrapCrafts* series

Editor: Cecilia C. Robinson
Editorial Assistant: Roslyn Oneille Hardy
Assistant Copy Editor: Susan Smith Cheatham
Production Manager: Rick Litton
Associate Production Manager: Theresa L. Beste
Production Assistant: Pam Beasley Bullock
Designer and Computer Artist: Larry Hunter
Additional Computer Art: Karen Tindall Tillery

CONTENTS

O HOLY NIGHT

The beloved Christmas story, symbolized by the crèche, is told here with shining beaded figures. The jewellike beading is stitched on perforated paper, a simple technique for such handsome ornaments. And on the following pages you'll discover soft-sculpture Wise Men and a trio of lace-trimmed angels, simple sewing projects that incorporate those lovely bits of trim you've saved for something spectacular.

BEADED CRÈCHE ORNAMENTS

MATERIALS (for 1)
- 2 completed bead designs on cream Perforated Paper 14
- Rubber cement
- Gold metallic thread
- Beading needle

DIRECTIONS

Construct ornament. Cut out each design along heavy lines indicated on graph. With wrong sides facing and edges aligned, glue front design piece to back. For hanger, sew a 6″ piece of gold metallic thread through top of ornament and knot ends together to make a loop.

Sample for Shepherd, Mary and Jesus, Joseph, and each Wise Man
Stitched on cream Perforated Paper 14 over 1, the finished design size is 1⅝″ x 3¼″. The paper was cut 4″ x 6″. Stitch 1 front and 1 back for each.

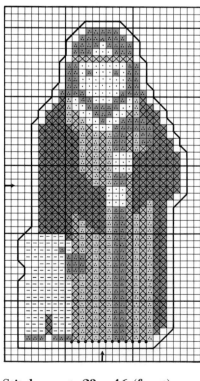

Stitch count: 23 x 46 (front)

SHEPHERD

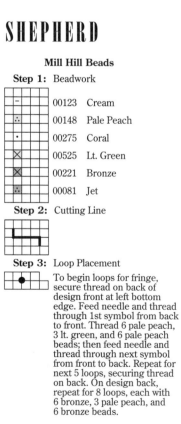

Mill Hill Beads

Step 1: Beadwork

−	00123	Cream
∴	00148	Pale Peach
•	00275	Coral
⊠	00525	Lt. Green
⊠	00221	Bronze
⦂	00081	Jet

Step 2: Cutting Line

Step 3: Loop Placement

To begin loops for fringe, secure thread on back of design front at left bottom edge. Feed needle and thread through 1st symbol from back to front. Thread 6 pale peach, 3 lt. green, and 6 pale peach beads; then feed needle and thread through next symbol from front to back. Repeat for next 5 loops, securing thread on back. On design back, repeat for 8 loops, each with 6 bronze, 3 pale peach, and 6 bronze beads.

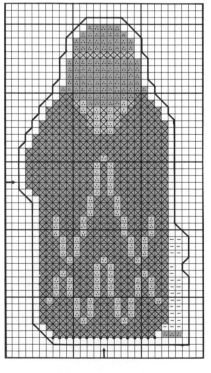

Stitch count: 23 x 46 (back)

ANGEL

Stitched on cream Perforated Paper 14 over 1, the finished design size is 1⅛" x 3¼". The paper was cut 4" x 6". Stitch 1 front and 1 back.

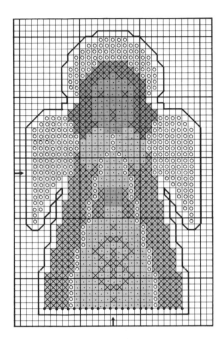

Stitch count: 27 x 45 (front)

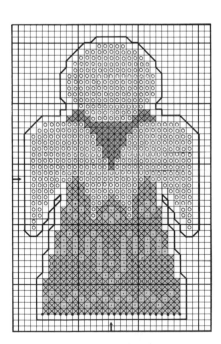

Stitch count: 27 x 45 (back)

Mill Hill Beads

Step 1: Beadwork

O	00557	Gold
.	00275	Coral
.	00146	Lt. Blue
X	00252	Iris
X	00081	Jet

Step 2: Cutting Line

Step 3: Loop Placement

To begin loops for fringe, secure thread on back of design front at left bottom edge. Feed needle and thread through 1st symbol from back to front. Thread 5 iris, 2 lt. blue, 1 gold, 2 lt. blue, and 5 iris beads; then feed needle and thread through next symbol from front to back. Repeat for next loop. For next 8 loops thread each with 5 lt. blue, 2 iris, 1 gold, 2 iris, and 5 lt. blue beads. For last 2 loops, repeat 1st 2 loops, securing thread on back. On design back, repeat for 12 loops, each with 5 iris, 2 lt. blue, 1 gold, 2 lt. blue, and 5 iris beads.

LAMB

Stitched on cream Perforated Paper 14 over 1, the finished design size is 1½" x 1½". The paper was cut 4" x 4". Stitch 1 front and 1 back.

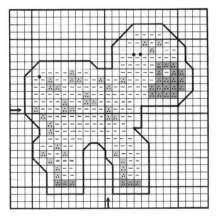

Stitch count: 21 x 21 (front)

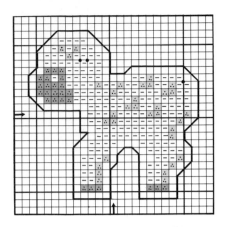

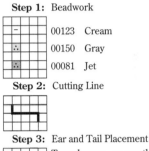

Stitch count: 21 x 21 (back)

Mill Hill Beads

Step 1: Beadwork

-	00123	Cream
.·	00150	Gray
.·	00081	Jet

Step 2: Cutting Line

Step 3: Ear and Tail Placement

To make ears, secure thread on back of design front at 1 symbol. Feed needle and thread through symbol from back to front. Thread 12 cream beads; then feed needle and thread through next symbol from front to back, securing thread on back. On design back, repeat for other ear.

Complete Directions before adding tail. To make tail, secure thread on 1 side of completed lamb at symbol, passing through lamb and exiting at symbol on other side. Thread 12 cream beads and feed needle and thread again through lamb at same symbol. Secure thread and clip close to beadwork.

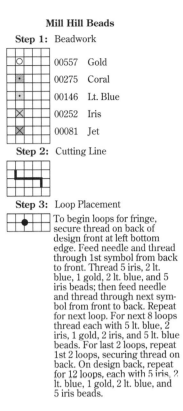

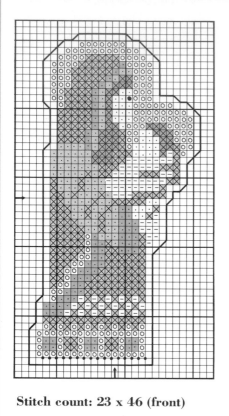

Stitch count: 23 x 46 (front)

MARY AND JESUS

(See sample on page 8)

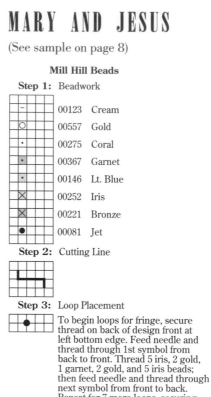

Mill Hill Beads

Step 1: Beadwork

−	00123	Cream
O	00557	Gold
·	00275	Coral
▪	00367	Garnet
·	00146	Lt. Blue
✕	00252	Iris
✕	00221	Bronze
●	00081	Jet

Step 2: Cutting Line

Step 3: Loop Placement

To begin loops for fringe, secure thread on back of design front at left bottom edge. Feed needle and thread through 1st symbol from back to front. Thread 5 iris, 2 gold, 1 garnet, 2 gold, and 5 iris beads; then feed needle and thread through next symbol from front to back. Repeat for 7 more loops, securing thread on back. Repeat for design back.

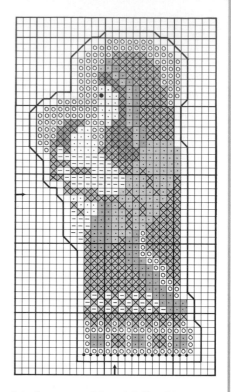

Stitch count: 23 x 46 (back)

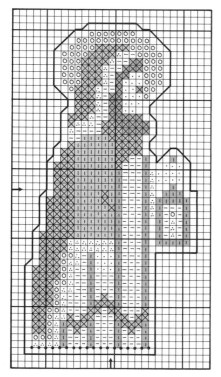

Stitch count: 23 x 46 (front)

JOSEPH

(See sample on page 8)

Mill Hill Beads

Step 1: Beadwork

−	00123	Cream
O	00557	Gold
·	00275	Coral
∴	00367	Garnet
ǀ	00525	Lt. Green
✕	00332	Emerald
▪	00221	Bronze
✕	00081	Jet

Step 2: Cutting Line

Step 3: Loop Placement

To begin loops for fringe, secure thread on back of design front at left bottom edge. Feed needle and thread through 1st symbol from back to front. Thread 5 bronze, 2 cream, 1 emerald, 2 cream, and 5 bronze beads; then feed needle and thread through next symbol from front to back. Repeat for 8 more loops, securing thread on back. Repeat for design back.

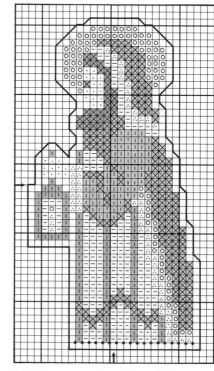

Stitch count: 23 x 46 (back)

DONKEY

Stitched on cream Perforated Paper 14 over 1, the finished design is 2⅞" x 3⅛". The paper was cut 5" x 6". Stitch 1 front and 1 back.

Mill Hill Beads

Step 1: Beadwork

–	00123	Cream
O	00557	Gold
+	00275	Coral
–	00367	Garnet
·	00332	Emerald
·	00150	Gray
●	00081	Jet

Step 2: Cutting Line

Step 3: Loop, Mane, and Tail Placement

To begin loops for blanket, secure thread on back of design front at left 1st symbol. Feed needle and thread through symbol from back to front. Thread 3 gold, 1 garnet, and 3 gold beads; then feed needle and thread through next symbol from front to back. For next 2 loops, repeat 1st loop, securing thread on back. On design back, repeat for 3 loops.

To make mane, secure thread on back of design front at left edge of head. Feed needle and thread through 1st symbol from back to front. Thread 12 jet beads; then feed needle and thread back through same symbol from front to back. Repeat for remaining 6 loops. On design back, repeat for 7 loops.

Complete Directions before adding tail. To make tail, secure thread on 1 side of completed donkey at 1 symbol, passing through donkey and exiting at symbol on other side. Thread 34 jet beads and feed needle and thread again through donkey at same symbol. Repeat for next loop, threading 24 jet beads. Secure thread and clip close to beadwork.

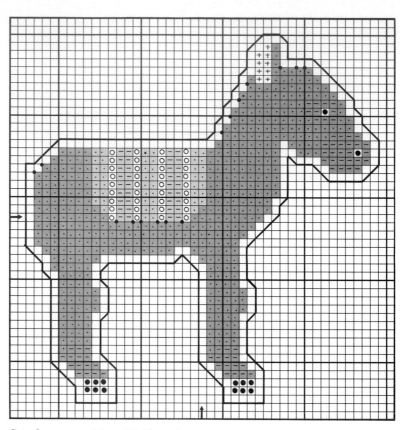

Stitch count: 41 x 43 (front)

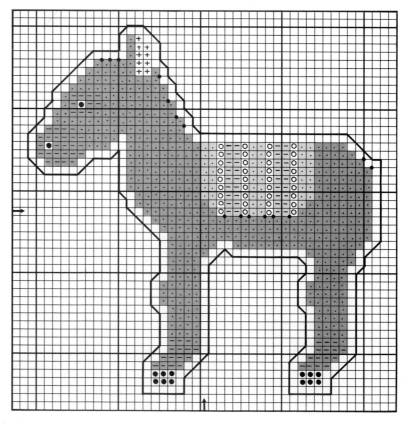

Stitch count: 41 x 43 (back)

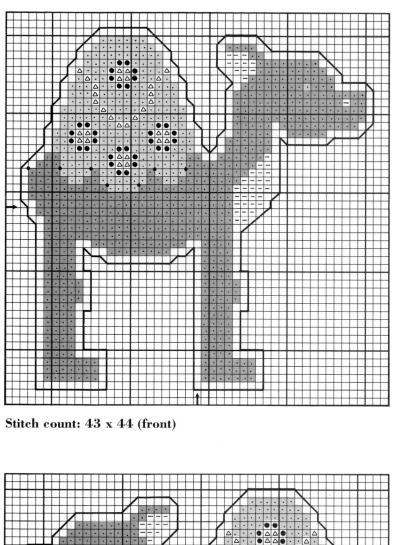

Stitch count: 43 x 44 (front)

Stitch count: 43 x 44 (back)

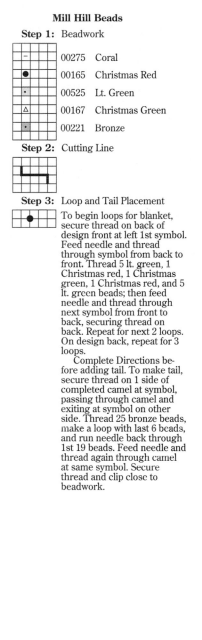

CAMEL

Stitched on cream Perforated Paper 14 over 1, the finished design size is 3⅛″ x 3⅛″. The paper was cut 6″ x 6″. Stitch 1 front and 1 back.

Mill Hill Beads

Step 1: Beadwork

−	00275	Coral
●	00165	Christmas Red
·	00525	Lt. Green
△	00167	Christmas Green
▨	00221	Bronze

Step 2: Cutting Line

Step 3: Loop and Tail Placement

To begin loops for blanket, secure thread on back of design front at left 1st symbol. Feed needle and thread through symbol from back to front. Thread 5 lt. green, 1 Christmas red, 1 Christmas green, 1 Christmas red, and 5 lt. green beads; then feed needle and thread through next symbol from front to back, securing thread on back. Repeat for next 2 loops. On design back, repeat for 3 loops.

Complete Directions before adding tail. To make tail, secure thread on 1 side of completed camel at symbol, passing through camel and exiting at symbol on other side. Thread 25 bronze beads, make a loop with last 6 beads, and run needle back through 1st 19 beads. Feed needle and thread again through camel at same symbol. Secure thread and clip close to beadwork.

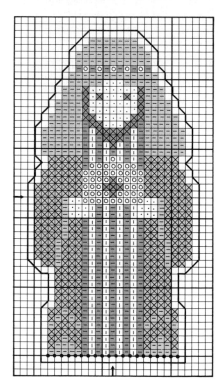

Stitch count: 23 x 46 (front)

GREEN WISE MAN

(See sample on page 8)

Mill Hill Beads

Step 1: Beadwork

I	00123	Cream
O	00557	Gold
·	00275	Coral
—	00367	Garnet
−	00525	Lt. Green
X	00167	Christmas Green
X	00081	Jet

Step 2: Cutting Line

Step 3: Loop Placement

To begin loops for fringe, secure thread on back of design front at left bottom edge. Feed needle and thread through 1st symbol from back to front. Thread 6 lt. green, 3 Christmas green, and 6 lt. green beads; then feed needle and thread through next symbol from front to back. Repeat for next 2 loops. For next 4 loops, thread each with 15 garnet beads. For last 3 loops, repeat 1st 3 loops, securing thread on back. On design back, repeat for 10 loops, each with 6 lt. green, 3 Christmas green, and 6 lt. green beads.

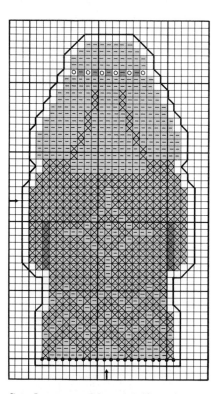

Stitch count: 23 x 46 (front)

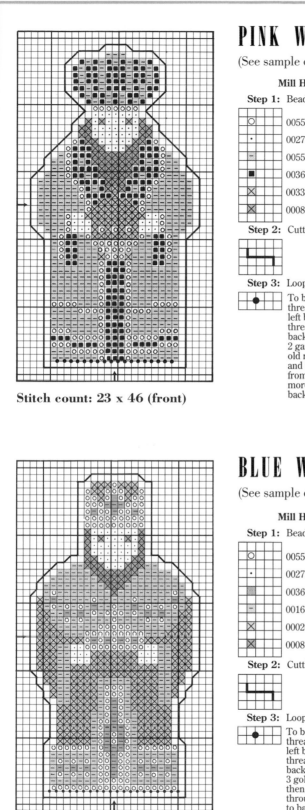

Stitch count: 23 x 46 (front)

PINK WISE MAN
(See sample on page 8)

Mill Hill Beads

Step 1: Beadwork

O	00557	Gold
·	00275	Coral
–	00553	Old Rose
■	00367	Garnet
✕	00332	Emerald
✕	00081	Jet

Step 2: Cutting Line

Step 3: Loop Placement

● To begin loops for fringe, secure thread on back of design front at left bottom edge. Feed needle and thread through 1st symbol from back to front. Thread 5 old rose, 2 garnet, 1 gold, 2 garnet, and 5 old rose beads; then feed needle and thread through next symbol from front to back. Repeat for 8 more loops, securing thread on back. Repeat for design back.

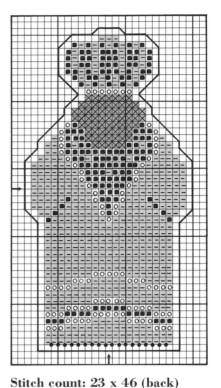

Stitch count: 23 x 46 (back)

Stitch count: 23 x 46 (front)

BLUE WISE MAN
(See sample on page 8)

Mill Hill Beads

Step 1: Beadwork

O	00557	Gold
·	00275	Coral
▨	00367	Garnet
–	00168	Sapphire
✕	00020	Royal Blue
✕	00081	Jet

Step 2: Cutting Line

Step 3: Loop Placement

● To begin loops for fringe, secure thread on back of design front at left bottom edge. Feed needle and thread through 1st symbol from back to front. Thread 6 royal blue, 3 gold, and 6 royal blue beads; then feed needle and thread through next symbol from front to back. Repeat for next 3 loops. For next 2 loops, thread each with 6 garnet, 3 gold, and 6 garnet beads. For last 4 loops, repeat 1st 4 loops, securing thread on back. On design back, repeat for 10 loops, each with 6 royal blue, 3 gold, and 6 royal blue beads.

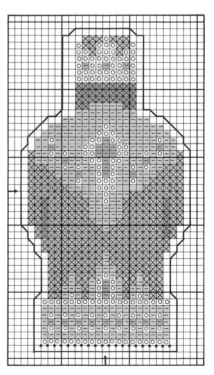

Stitch count: 23 x 46 (back)

WE THREE KINGS

MATERIALS FOR EACH:
- Patterns on page 134
- Scrap of muslin
- Thread: white and gold metallic
- 2 black glass seed beads
- 1 (⁵⁄₁₆″-long) pink bugle bead
- Beading needle
- Large embroidery needle
- Stuffing

For green wise man:
- Scrap of green velveteen
- Green thread
- ½ yard (⁵⁄₁₆″-wide) gold metallic trim
- 1 yard (1″-wide) black cotton lace
- 6½″ (1½″-wide) black floral trim
- 3 (⅞″) black-and-gold crown buttons
- Scrap of 3-ply black yarn
- 5½″ (¾″-wide) gold metallic trim

For blue wise man:
- Scrap of blue velveteen
- Blue thread
- 4 (6½″) lengths of ¼″-wide purple corded braid
- 6½″ (1⅜″-wide) print trim
- ½ yard (¾″-wide) gold metallic trim
- ½ yard (⅛″-wide) turquoise rayon cording
- 1 (⁵⁄₁₆″) turquoise glass bead
- Scrap of 3-ply black yarn

For burgundy wise man:
- Scrap of burgundy velveteen
- Burgundy thread
- 13″ (¾″-wide) gold metallic trim
- 6½″ (1¾″-wide) multicolored metallic trim
- 4 (⁵⁄₁₆″) gold ball buttons
- ¼ yard of pink metallic lamé
- Scrap of 3-ply brown yarn
- ¼ yard of blue metallic lamé
- 1 (⁵⁄₁₆″) rhinestone button

DIRECTIONS
Patterns include ¼″ seam allowance.

1. Prepare materials. For each: Transfer patterns for body and face and cut out as indicated.

2. Make body front. For each: With right sides up and outer edges aligned, place face on body as indicated on pattern. Satin-stitch through both layers along raw neck edge. Sew black beads for eyes and bugle bead for mouth to face. **For green wise man:** Cut 2 (6½″) lengths of gold trim and 2 (6½″) lengths of black lace. Sew 1 black lace length to each long edge of black floral trim. Center and stitch 1 length of gold metallic trim over each seam. Center embellished trim vertically on right side of body front below neck; baste. Referring to photo, sew buttons to trim. **For blue wise man:** Sew 1 braid length to each long edge of print trim. Center embellished trim vertically on right side of body front below neck; baste. Referring to photo and beginning at neck edge of print trim, stitch 1 purple braid length to each side of body front at an angle, ending at bottom corner of body. **For burgundy wise man:** Cut gold trim in half. Stitch 1 length to each long edge of multicolored metallic trim. Center embellished trim vertically on right side of body front below neck; baste. Referring to photo, sew buttons to trim.

3. Complete body. For each: With right sides facing, sew body front to body back, leaving open as indicated on pattern. Clip curves, turn, and stuff firmly. Slipstitch opening closed. **For green wise man:** For collar, run a gathering thread along 1 edge of remaining black lace. Pull to gather collar to fit neck. Tack collar around neck above satin stitching. Tack remaining gold trim around neck above black lace. **For blue wise man:** For collar, cut 1 (12″) length of gold trim and run a gathering thread along 1 edge. Pull to gather collar to fit neck. Tack collar around neck above satin stitching. Thread both ends of turquoise cording through turquoise bead, making a loop, and place cording around neck. Sew cording together approximately 2″ below neck. Pull bead up to cover stitching. Knot cording 1″ from each end and unravel ends. **For burgundy wise man:** For collar, fold pink lamé lengthwise into thirds, with long raw edges inside fold. Tack 1 end to center back of neck. Twist and tack pink lamé around neck, ending in back. Turn raw end under ¼″ and tack.

4. Complete ornament. For green and blue wise men: For hair, make small loops with black yarn and stitch around edges of face. To make a crown, tack 1 (5½″) length of gold trim around head, overlapping ends at back, and secure. **For burgundy wise man:** For hair, make small loops with brown yarn and stitch around edges of face. For turban, fold blue lamé lengthwise into thirds, with long raw edges inside fold. Tack 1 end to back of head. Wrap lamé around head ¼″ above eyes, coiling in a loose turban. Tuck raw end inside wraps and tack to secure. Tack rhinestone button to center front of turban. **For each:** For hanger, sew a 10″ piece of gold metallic thread through top back of head and knot ends together to make a loop.

VELVETEEN ANGELS

MATERIALS FOR EACH:
- Patterns on page 135
- Scrap of muslin
- Thread: white, gold metallic
- 2 light blue seed beads
- 1 (³⁄₁₆″-long) red bugle bead
- Beading needle
- Stuffing
- Scrap of 3-ply pale yellow yarn

For pink angel:
- Scrap of pink velveteen
- 6″ (5½″-wide) white lace for dress front
- Pink thread
- Small pearl beads
- ⅛″-wide clear sequins
- ½ yard (1¼″-wide) white lace for collar
- 28″ (1⅜″-wide) white trim with pink design for wings

For blue angel:
- Scrap of light blue velveteen
- Light blue thread
- 6½″ (2″-wide) white trim with blue design for dress front
- ½ yard (1⅛″-wide) white lace for collar
- 1⅛ yards (1⅜″-wide) white trim with blue design for wings

For peach angel:
- Scrap of peach velveteen
- Peach thread
- 6½″ (2″-wide) cream trim with peach design for dress front
- ½ yard (1″-wide) cream lace for collar
- 28″ (1½″-wide) cream trim for wings

DIRECTIONS
Patterns include ¼″ seam allowance.

1. Prepare materials. For each: Transfer patterns for face and body and cut out as indicated. **For pink angel:** Transfer bottom of body pattern (from face placement line down) to 5½″-wide lace piece and cut 1.

2. Make body. For each: With pieces right sides up and outer edges aligned, place face on body as indicated on pattern. Satin-stitch through both layers along raw neck edge. Sew light blue beads for eyes and bugle bead for mouth to face. **For pink angel:** With right sides up and raw edges aligned, place lace body piece on body front below neck; baste. **For blue and peach angels:** Center 2″-wide trim vertically on right side of body front below neck and stitch in place. **For each:** With right sides facing, sew body front to body back, leaving open as indicated on pattern. Turn and stuff firmly; slipstitch opening closed.

3. Embellish ornament. For pink angel: Sew pearl beads and sequins to 1¼″-wide lace piece as desired. **For each:** For collar, run a gathering thread along straight edge of lace piece. Pull to gather collar to fit neck. Tack collar to body above neck satin stitching. For hair, make small loops of yarn and stitch around edges of face.

4. Complete ornament. For pink and peach angels: For wings, cut trim in half and sew ends of each length together to make 2 loops. With seam centered at back, tack center of each loop to center back of angel 1½″ from top of head. **For blue angel:** For wings, cut blue design trim into thirds and sew ends of each length together to make 3 loops. Attach wings to angel as above. **For each:** For hanger, sew a 10″ piece of metallic thread through top back of head and knot ends together to make a loop.

Decorate your front porch wreath with this celestial trio for a glorious welcome to holiday visitors.

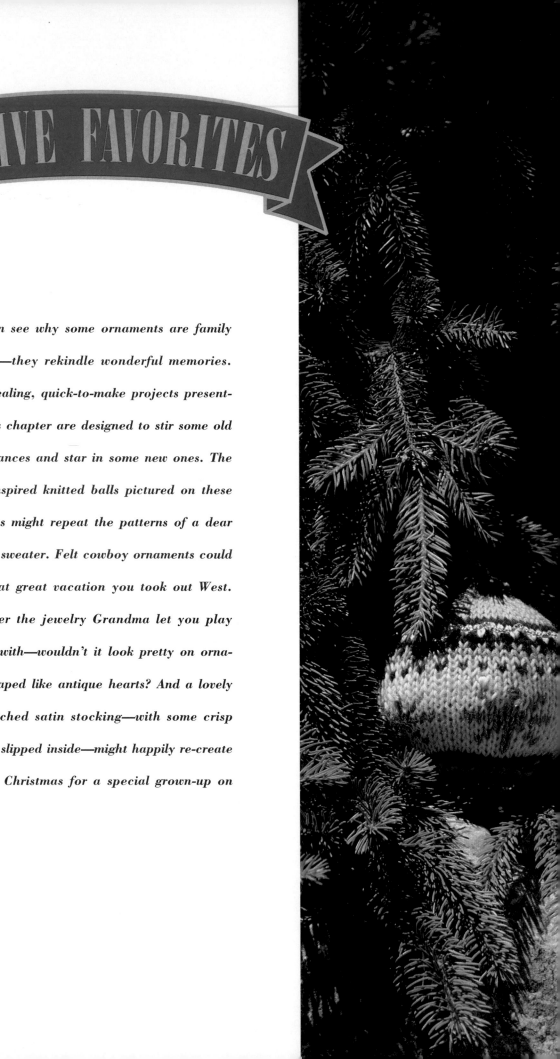

FESTIVE FAVORITES

Y ou can see why some ornaments are family favorites—they rekindle wonderful memories. The appealing, quick-to-make projects presented in this chapter are designed to stir some old remembrances and star in some new ones. The Nordic-inspired knitted balls pictured on these two pages might repeat the patterns of a dear Fair Isle sweater. Felt cowboy ornaments could recall that great vacation you took out West. Remember the jewelry Grandma let you play dress-up with—wouldn't it look pretty on ornaments shaped like antique hearts? And a lovely cross-stitched satin stocking—with some crisp new bills slipped inside—might happily re-create a child's Christmas for a special grown-up on your list.

SNOWFLAKE

MATERIALS

- DMC Tapestry Wool (8-yd. skein) (see color code)
- 4 (size 3) double-pointed knitting needles
- 1 spool of silver Balger blending filament
- Stitch markers
- 1 package of silver glass seed beads
- White thread
- Beading needle
- 4″-diameter craft foam ball

DIRECTIONS

Note: Knitting abbreviations are on page 160.

1. Knit ornament cover. Gauge: 5 sts = 1″, 6 rnds = 1″. (*Note:* Read chart from right to left, repeating indicated portion as necessary. To change colors, wrap old yarn over new so no holes occur. To inc, k into front and back of st. Add 1 strand of silver Balger thread to light blue yarn for snowflakes.) *Rnd 1:* With navy blue, cast 5 sts onto 3 needles. *Rnd 2:* Inc 1 in ea st around = 10 sts. *Rnd 3:* Inc 1 in ea st around = 20 sts. *Rnd 4:* * Inc 1, k 2, inc 1, place marker on needle (= 1 rep of chart), rep from * 4 times more. *Rnd 5:* K around. Cut yarn. *Rnd 6:* With white, * inc 1, k 4, inc 1, rep from * around = 40 sts. Cut yarn. *Rnds 7–8:* With light blue, k around. Cut yarn after rnd 8. *Rnd 9:* With yellow, * inc 1, k 6, inc 1, rep from * around = 50 sts. *Rnd 10:* Join red and k 1, pick up yellow and k 1, continue around as est. Cut yellow yarn. *Rnd 11:* Continue with red, * inc 1, k 8, inc 1, rep from * around = 60 sts. Cut yarn. *Rnds 12–42:* K ea rnd, changing colors as indicated on chart. *Rnd 43:* Bind off loosely, leaving a 12″ tail of yarn. Thread tail through remaining sts. Pull up tightly and secure. Weave in yarn ends.

2. Complete ornament. With white thread and beading needle, secure thread behind 1 st of white yarn on rnd 6, thread 6 beads, sk 1½ sts and stitch under ½ st. Repeat around rnd 6, threading 6 beads in each loop = 20 loops, and cut thread. Secure thread behind 1 st on last rnd of white yarn at top of ornament, thread 14 beads, sk 3 sts and stitch under ½ st. Repeat around last rnd of white yarn, threading 14 beads in each loop = 17 loops, and cut thread. Insert craft foam ball in knit covering. Pull up tightly on tail of yarn and secure. For hanger, sew a 10″ length of light blue yarn through top of ornament and knot ends together to make a loop.

DMC Tapestry Wool

Step 1: Knit (1 strand)

Symbol	Code	Color
–		White
⋰	7504	Old Gold-lt.
O	7666	Christmas Red
△	7313	Baby Blue-lt.
⋰	7313	Baby Blue-lt. + Silver Metallic
✕	7319	Royal Blue

TREE

MATERIALS

- DMC Tapestry Wool (8-yd. skein) (see color code)
- Aarlan Charmeuse yarn (185-yd. skein) (see color code)
- 4 (size 3) double-pointed knitting needles
- Stitch markers
- 120 gold glass seed beads
- Green thread
- Beading needle
- 4″-diameter craft foam ball

DIRECTIONS

Note: Knitting abbreviations are on page 160.

1. Knit ornament cover. Gauge: 5 sts = 1″, 6 rnds = 1″. (*Note:* Read chart from right to left, repeating indicated portion as necessary. To change colors, wrap old yarn over new so no holes occur. To inc, k into front and back of st. When working with Aarlan Charmeuse, use 2 strands held tog as 1.) *Rnd 1:* With blue, cast 5 sts onto 3 needles. *Rnd 2:* Inc 1 in ea st around = 10 sts.

Rnd 3: Inc 1 in ea st around = 20 sts. *Rnd 4:* * Inc 1, k 2, inc 1, place marker on needle (= 1 rep of chart), rep from * 4 times more. *Rnd 5:* K around. Cut yarn. *Rnd 6:* With red, * inc 1, k 4, inc 1, rep from * around = 40 sts. Cut yarn. *Rnds 7–8:* With DMC green, k around. Cut yarn after rnd 8. *Rnd 9:* With white, * inc 1, k 6, inc 1, rep from * around = 50 sts. Cut yarn. *Rnd 10:* With red, * inc 1, k 8, inc 1, rep from * around = 60 sts. *Rnds 11–42:* K ea rnd, changing colors as indicated on chart. *Rnd 43:* Bind off loosely, leaving a 12″ tail of yarn. Thread tail through remaining sts. Pull up tightly and secure. Weave in yarn ends.

2. Complete ornament. With green thread and beading needle, stitch gold beads to trees as indicated on chart. Insert craft foam ball in knit covering. Pull up tightly on tail of yarn and secure. For hanger, sew a 10″ length of red yarn through top of ornament and knot ends together to make a loop. (Use a clean toothbrush to fluff green yarn of trees.)

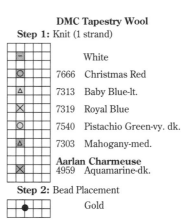

DMC Tapestry Wool

Step 1: Knit (1 strand)

−		White
O	7666	Christmas Red
△	7313	Baby Blue-lt.
✕	7319	Royal Blue
O	7540	Pistachio Green-vy. dk.
△	7303	Mahogany-med.

Aarlan Charmeuse
| ✕ | 4959 | Aquamarine-dk. |

Step 2: Bead Placement

| ● | | Gold |

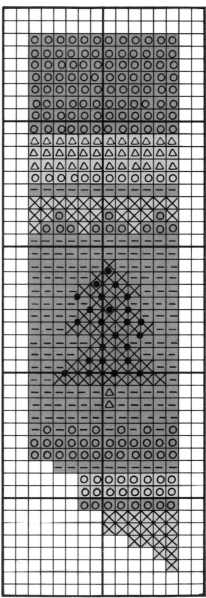

STAR

MATERIALS

- DMC Tapestry Wool (8-yd. skein) (see color code)
- 4 (size 3) double-pointed knitting needles
- 1 spool of gold Balger blending filament
- Stitch markers
- 1 package of gold glass seed beads
- White thread
- Beading needle
- 4″-diameter craft foam ball

DIRECTIONS

Note: Knitting abbreviations are on page 160.

Knit ornament cover. Gauge: 5 sts = 1″, 6 rnds = 1″. (*Note:* Read chart from right to left, repeating indicated portion as necessary. To change colors, wrap old yarn over new so no holes occur. To inc, k into front and back of st. Add 1 strand of gold Balger thread to yellow yarn for stars.) *Rnd 1:* With light blue, cast 5 sts onto 3 needles. *Rnd 2:* Inc 1 in ea st around = 10 sts. *Rnd 3:* Inc 1 in ea st around = 20 sts. *Rnd 4:* * Inc 1, k 2, inc 1, place marker on needle (= 1

rep of chart), rep from * 4 times more. *Rnd 5:* K around. *Rnd 6:* * Inc 1, k 4, inc 1, rep from * around = 40 sts. Cut yarn. *Rnds 7–8:* With yellow, k around. Cut yarn after rnd 8. *Rnd 9:* With navy blue, * inc 1, k 6, inc 1, rep from * around = 50 sts. Cut yarn. *Rnd 10:* With white, * inc 1, k 8, inc 1, rep from * around = 60 sts. *Rnds 11–42:* Join red and k ea rnd, changing colors as indicated on chart. *Rnd 43:* Bind off loosely, leaving a 12″ tail of yarn. Thread tail through remaining sts. Pull up tightly and secure. Weave in yarn ends.

2. Complete ornament. With white thread and beading needle, secure thread behind 1 st of yellow yarn on rnd 7, thread 6 beads, sk 1½ sts and stitch under ½ st. Repeat around rnd 6, threading 6 beads in each loop = 21 loops, and cut thread. Secure thread behind 1 st on first rnd of yellow yarn above stars, thread 14 beads, sk 3 sts and stitch under ½ st. Repeat around this rnd of yellow yarn, threading 14 beads in each loop = 30 loops, and cut thread. Insert craft foam ball in knit covering. Pull up tightly on tail of yarn and secure. For hanger, sew a 10″ length of yellow

yarn through top of ornament and knot ends together to make a loop.

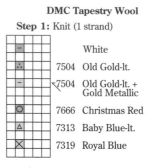

DMC Tapestry Wool

Step 1: Knit (1 strand)

−	White
∴	7504 Old Gold-lt.
−	7504 Old Gold-lt. + Gold Metallic
○	7666 Christmas Red
△	7313 Baby Blue-lt.
✕	7319 Royal Blue

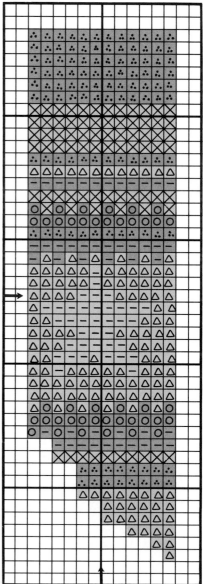

SNOWMAN

MATERIALS
- DMC Tapestry Wool (8-yd. skein) (see color code)
- Aarlan Charmeuse yarn (185-yd. skein) (see color code)
- 4 (size 3) double-pointed knitting needles
- Stitch markers
- 15 (3-mm) gold ball beads
- 15 (2-mm) black glass beads
- White thread
- Beading needle
- 4"-diameter craft foam ball
- 10 (1½"-long) forked twigs

DIRECTIONS
Note: Knitting abbreviations are on page 160.

1. Knit ornament cover. Gauge: 5 sts = 1", 6 rnds = 1". (*Note:* Read chart from right to left, repeating indicated portion as necessary. To change colors, wrap old yarn over new so no holes occur. To inc, k into front and back of st. When working with Aarlan Charmeuse, use 2 strands held tog as 1.) *Rnd 1:* With green, cast 5 sts onto 3 needles. *Rnd 2:* Inc 1 in ea st around = 10 sts. *Rnd 3:* Inc 1 in ea st around = 20 sts.

Rnd 4: * Inc 1, k 2, inc 1, place marker on needle (= 1 rep of chart), rep from * 4 times more. *Rnd 5:* K around. Cut yarn. *Rnd 6:* With DMC white, * inc 1, k 4, inc 1, rep from * around = 40 sts. Cut yarn. *Rnds 7–8:* With red, k around. Cut yarn after rnd 8. *Rnd 9:* With DMC white, * inc 1, k 6, inc 1, repeat from * around = 50 sts. Cut yarn. *Rnd 10:* With green, * inc 1, k 8, inc 1, rep from * around = 60 sts. *Rnd 11:* K around. *Rnd 12:* Join blue and k 1, pick up green and k 1, continue around as est. *Rnds 13–42:* K ea rnd, changing colors as indicated on chart. *Rnd 43:* Bind off loosely, leaving a 12" tail of yarn. Thread tail through remaining sts. Pull up tightly and secure. Weave in yarn ends.

2. Complete ornament. With white thread and beading needle, stitch 3 gold and 3 black beads to each snowman as indicated on chart. For hat brims, make a straightstitch with red as indicated on chart. Insert craft foam ball in knit covering. Pull up tightly on tail of yarn and secure. For hanger, sew a 10" length of green yarn through top of ornament and knot ends together to make a loop. Tack twig arms to snowmen as indicated on

chart. (Use a clean toothbrush to fluff white yarn of snowmen.)

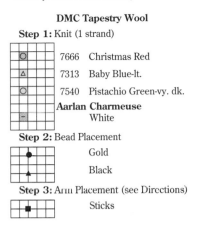

DMC Tapestry Wool
Step 1: Knit (1 strand)

⊙	7666 Christmas Red
△	7313 Baby Blue-lt.
○	7540 Pistachio Green-vy. dk.

Aarlan Charmeuse
White (—)

Step 2: Bead Placement

●	Gold
▲	Black

Step 3: Arm Placement (see Directions)

■	Sticks

SANTA'S FACE

MATERIALS
- Pattern on page 134
- Completed cross-stitch on white Linda 27
- 3″-diameter craft foam ball
- Paring knife
- Scrap of red velvet
- Scraps of white artificial fur
- Thread: red, white, gold metallic
- Craft glue
- Small amount of stuffing
- 1 package of white filament fiber curly hair

DIRECTIONS
Pattern includes ¼″ seam allowance. All seam allowances are ¼″.

1. Prepare materials. Mark a line around center of craft foam ball to divide it in half. Using paring knife, score a ¼″-deep line. (Keep score line as narrow and inconspicuous as possible.) Transfer hat pattern and cut as indicated. From fur, cut 1 (2½″ x 11½″) piece for hat trim and 1 (2½″-diameter) circle for pom-pom.

2. Cover ball. Center design piece over ½ of ball. Using knife, poke edges of fabric into score line. Make small tucks as needed to mold fabric smoothly over round surface. Trim excess fabric close to ball.

3. Make hat. With right sides facing and raw edges aligned, fold hat in half lengthwise. Stitch long straight edge. Turn. Place hat on back half of ball. Glue edges of hat to ball near score line. To make pom-pom, run a gathering thread along raw edge of circle and pull to gather. Stuff and gather tightly; secure threads. Tack to point of hat. To make trim, with right sides facing and raw edges aligned, fold hat trim strip in half lengthwise. Stitch long edge. Turn. Place trim around ball to cover score line and edge of hat.

Glue trim in place, overlapping ends in back.

4. Attach beard and hair. Apply thin coat of glue to unstitched fabric outside edges of cross-stitch design. Glue curly hair as desired for beard and hair. Glue small piece of curly hair under nose for mustache.

5. Complete ornament. Referring to photo, fold point of hat to 1 side and glue or pin in place. To make hanger, cut 1 (24″) length of gold metallic thread. Fold in half and thread needle with double thickness of thread. Take a stitch through hat just above trim and knot ends together to make a loop.

Sample for Santa's Face
Stitched on white Linda 27 over 2 threads, the finished design size is 2¼″ x 2½″. The fabric was cut 7″ x 7″.

Anchor			DMC	(used for sample)
Step 1: Cross-stitch (2 strands)				
1	–			White
4146	·	╱	754	Peach-lt.
868	△	╱	758	Terra Cotta-lt.
8	▬	╱	761	Salmon-lt.
9	○	╱	760	Salmon
130	○	╱	799	Delft-med.
397	–	╱	762	Pearl Gray-vy. lt.
398	∴	╱	415	Pearl Gray
236	●		3799	Pewter Gray-vy. dk.
Step 2: Backstitch (1 strand)				
355			975	Golden Brown-dk. (eyes, nose, bottom of mouth, face outline)
400			414	Steel Gray-dk. (eyebrows, bottom of mustache, top of mouth)
236			3799	Pewter Gray-vy. dk. (around pupils)

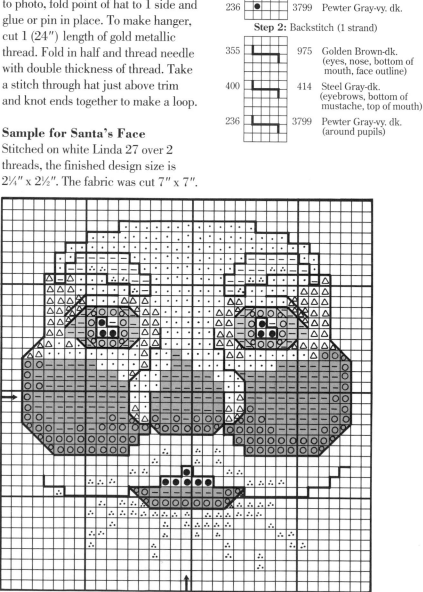

Stitch count: 31 x 33

WHITE SATIN STOCKING

MATERIALS
- Pattern on page 137
- Completed cross-stitch on white Murano 30
- ⅛ yard of white satin fabric
- Scrap of flannel
- 2 yards (¹⁄₁₆″-wide) dark green rayon cord
- 7″ (⅛″-wide) dark red rayon cord
- Liquid ravel preventer
- Thread: white, dark green

DIRECTIONS
Pattern includes ¼″ seam allowance.

1. Prepare materials. With design in upper-right quarter, trim Murano to 6″ x 5½″ (see Diagram). From satin, cut 1 (2½″ x 1¼″) piece for hanger. Transfer stocking pattern to remaining satin and cut 4. Transfer stocking pattern to flannel and cut 2. Cut 2 (7″) and 2 (10″) lengths from green cord.

Apply liquid ravel preventer to ends of all green and red cord lengths.

2. Make stocking. Pin flannel stocking pieces to wrong sides of 2 satin stocking pieces. With right sides facing and raw edges aligned, stitch pieces together around side and bottom edges, leaving top edge open. Trim flannel from seam, clip curves, and turn. To make cuff, with right

sides facing and raw edges aligned, fold design piece in half widthwise and stitch 5½″ edges together. With wrong sides facing and long raw edges aligned, fold cuff in half lengthwise; baste top raw edges together. With design side out, top raw edges aligned, and seam centered at back, place cuff over stocking; baste. To make hanger loop, with right sides facing and raw edges aligned, fold 2½″ x 1¼″ piece of satin in half lengthwise and stitch long edges together. Turn. Fold in half with raw ends aligned. Referring to photo for placement, pin to top right of stocking back. For lining, with right sides

facing and raw edges aligned, stitch remaining stocking pieces together around side and bottom edges, leaving top edge open and a 2″ opening above heel. Clip curves. Do not turn. With right sides facing and top edges and seams aligned, slide lining over stocking. Stitch around top edge of stocking, catching cuff and loop in seam. Turn through opening in lining; slipstitch opening closed. Tuck lining inside stocking.

3. Trim cuff. With matching thread, tack 1 (7″) length of green cord around cuff above design and 1 below

design (see photo). Knot ends of red cord and 10″ lengths of green cord together. Referring to photo, wrap green cords around red cord, making a loose X pattern, and tack to cuff. Continue wrapping and tacking cords to cuff. Cut remaining green cord into 3 equal pieces. Braid cord and tack to bottom edge of cuff.

Sample for Stocking
Stitched on white Murano 30 over 2 threads, the finished design size is 2¾″ x 1⅝″. The fabric was cut 7½″ x 8″. Begin stitching center of design 5″ from left edge and 2¾″ from top edge of fabric.

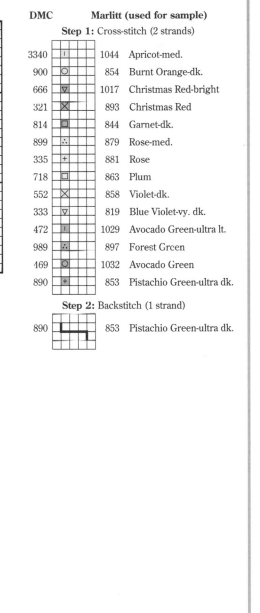

DMC		Marlitt (used for sample)	
Step 1: Cross-stitch (2 strands)			
3340	I	1044	Apricot-med.
900	O	854	Burnt Orange-dk.
666	▽	1017	Christmas Red-bright
321	X	893	Christmas Red
814	□	844	Garnet-dk.
899	∴	879	Rose-med.
335	+	881	Rose
718	□	863	Plum
552	X	858	Violet-dk.
333	▽	819	Blue Violet-vy. dk.
472	I	1029	Avocado Green-ultra lt.
989	∴	897	Forest Green
469	O	1032	Avocado Green
890	+	853	Pistachio Green-ultra dk.
Step 2: Backstitch (1 strand)			
890	⌐	853	Pistachio Green-ultra dk.

Stitch count: 42 x 24

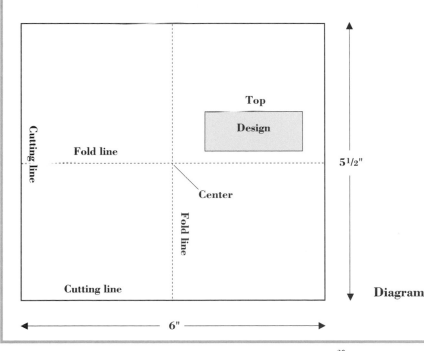

TAPESTRY WREATHS

MATERIALS (for 1)
- Completed cross-stitch design on cream Belfast Linen 32
- 3¼″-diameter circle of matching fabric for back
- 4″ x 8″ piece of satin fabric
- 12″ (⅛″) cording
- ¾ yard (¹⁄₁₆″-wide) green, pink, or purple satin ribbon
- Small amount of stuffing
- Tapestry needle

DIRECTIONS
All seam allowances are ¼″.

1. Prepare materials. With design centered, trim design piece to a 3¼″-diameter circle. Cut a 1″-diameter circle from center of design piece and back piece. Cut 1″-wide bias strips from satin fabric, piecing as needed to equal 12″; with cording, make 12″ of corded piping. Cut cording into 1 (2″) and 1 (10″) length.

2. Make wreath. With right sides facing and raw edges aligned, stitch 10″ length of piping around outer edge of design piece. Repeat with 2″ length of piping around inner circle. With right sides facing and raw edges aligned, stitch outer edges of design piece to back piece along stitching line of piping. Turn. Turn edge of inner circle under ¼″ and slipstitch a short distance; do not cut thread; stuff firmly inside stitched area. Continue to slipstitch and stuff until ornament is completed. Cut 2 (14″) lengths of ribbon and tie each length in a bow. Tack bows together at top of ornament. For hanger, thread tapestry needle with remaining ribbon and sew through top of ornament. Knot ends together to make a loop.

Add one of these bright, colorful wreaths to a package wrap for a personal touch with flair.

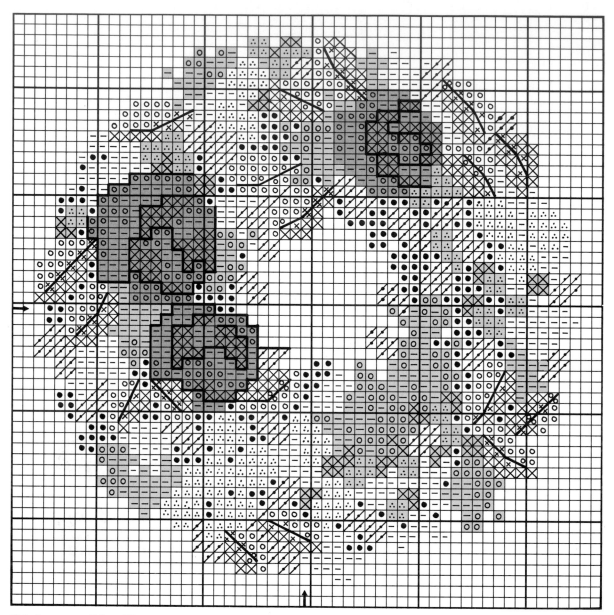

Stitch count: 51 x 51

PINK WREATH

Stitched on cream Belfast Linen 32
over 2 threads, the finished design
size is 3¼" x 3¼". The fabric was cut
6" x 6".

Anchor		DMC	(used for sample)

Step 1: Cross-stitch (2 strands)

Anchor		DMC	
890	−	729	Old Gold-med.
11	−	351	Coral
13	⊙	349	Coral-dk.
66	∴	3688	Mauve-med.
77	∴	602	Cranberry-med.
59	✕	600	Cranberry-vy. dk.
47	✕	304	Christmas Red-med.
88	○	718	Plum
98	−	553	Violet-med.
843	○	3364	Pine Green

Anchor		DMC	
861	✕	3363	Pine Green-med.
246	╱	319	Pistachio Green-vy. dk.
879	●	500	Blue Green-vy. dk.

Step 2: Backstitch (1 strand)

Anchor		DMC	
47		304	Christmas Red-med. (flowers)
879		500	Blue Green-vy. dk. (stems)

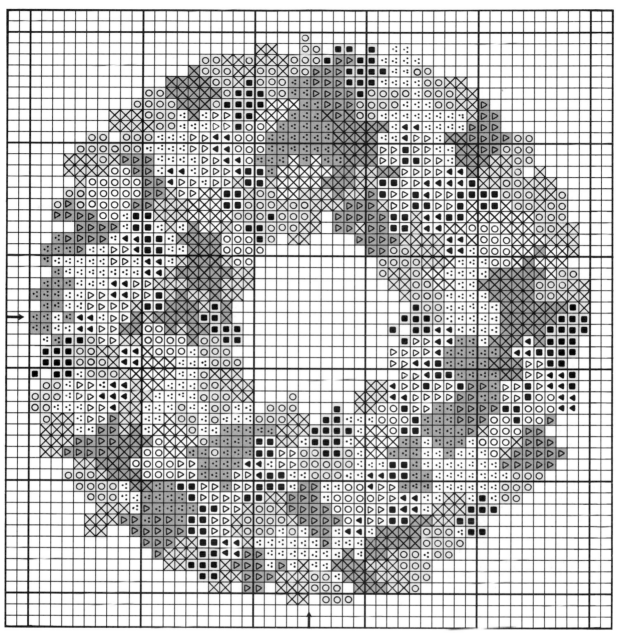

Stitch count: 50 x 51

GREEN WREATH

Stitched on cream Belfast Linen 32 over 2 threads, the finished design size is 3¼″ x 3⅛″. The fabric was cut 6″ x 6″.

Anchor		DMC (used for sample)					
		Step 1: Cross-stitch (2 strands)					
886	∴	677	Old Gold-vy. lt.	119	⊠	333	Blue Violet-vy. dk.
306	○	725	Topaz	216	⊙	320	Pistachio Green-med.
890	⊠	729	Old Gold-med.	246	⊠	319	Pistachio Green-vy. dk.
11	▷	351	Coral	349	▷	301	Mahogany-med.
13	◄	349	Coral-dk.	379	■	840	Beige Brown-med.
47	■	304	Christmas Red-med.				
98	∷	553	Violet-med.				

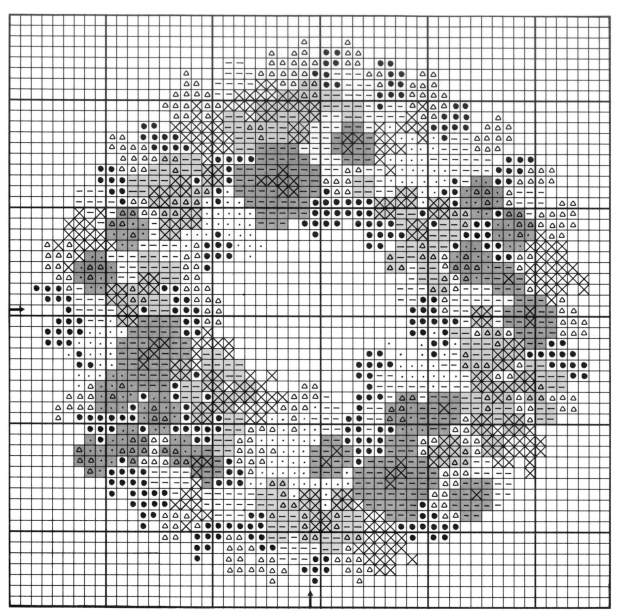

Stitch count: 52 x 51

PURPLE WREATH

Stitched on cream Belfast Linen 32
over 2 threads, the finished design
size is 3¼″ x 3¼″. The fabric was cut
6″ x 6″.

Anchor		DMC (used for sample)	
		Step 1: Cross-stitch (2 strands)	

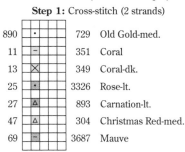

Anchor			DMC	
890	·		729	Old Gold-med.
11	−		351	Coral
13	✕		349	Coral-dk.
25	·		3326	Rose-lt.
27	△		893	Carnation-lt.
47	△		304	Christmas Red-med.
69	−		3687	Mauve

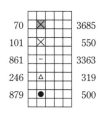

Anchor			DMC	
70	✕		3685	Mauve-dk.
101	✕		550	Violet-vy. dk.
861	−		3363	Pine Green-med.
246	△		319	Pistachio Green-vy. dk.
879	●		500	Blue Green-vy. dk.

COWBOY SANTA

MATERIALS
- Patterns on page 136
- 2 (5″) squares of white felt
- Felt scraps: tan, light pink, rose, red
- Scrap of craft fleece
- 12″ (⅛″-wide) red grosgrain ribbon
- 6″ (⅛″-wide) green grosgrain ribbon
- Craft glue
- Thread to match fabrics
- 1 (⅜″) red faceted plastic heart
- 2 (⅜″) blue faceted plastic hearts

DIRECTIONS
1. Prepare materials. Transfer patterns and cut out as indicated. Cut green ribbon into 3 (2″) lengths.

2. Assemble Santa. For ornament back, glue 1 hat piece to 1 head piece. Using hat/head piece as pattern, cut 1 from fleece and trim fleece piece ⅛″ smaller than pattern. For hanger, fold red ribbon in half and glue fold to wrong side of hat piece as indicated on pattern. For ornament front, glue cheeks, mouth, and then face to wrong side of head front. Glue remaining hat piece and nose to right side of ornament front. With raw edges aligned, stack ornament back (right side down), fleece, and ornament front (right side up). With matching thread, whipstitch all edges together, catching hanger in stitching. Knot ends of hanger together to make a loop.

3. Embellish Santa. Glue 1 green ribbon length across front of hat (see photo) and 1 to back of hat for hatband. Fold remaining ribbon length in half and, referring to photo, glue fold to front of hatband. Glue red heart over fold and blue hearts to face for eyes.

COWBOY BOOT

MATERIALS
- Patterns on page 137
- 2 (5″) squares of red felt
- Felt scraps: white, green
- Scrap of craft fleece
- 24″ (⅛″-wide) green grosgrain ribbon
- Craft glue
- Red thread
- 2 (⅜″) red faceted plastic hearts

DIRECTIONS
1. Prepare materials. Transfer patterns and cut out as indicated. Trim edges of fleece boot piece ⅛″ smaller than pattern. Cut along short solid lines of fringe piece for fringe. Cut ribbon into 1 (12″) length and 4 (3″) lengths.

2. Assemble boot. For hanger, fold 12″ length of ribbon in half and glue fold to wrong side of 1 boot as indicated on pattern. With raw edges aligned, stack boot piece with hanger (right side down), fleece, and remaining boot piece. With matching thread, whipstitch edges of boot pieces together, catching hanger in stitching.

3. Embellish boot. Glue 1 fringe piece ½″ below top edge on each side of boot. Referring to photo for placement, glue 2 (3″) ribbon lengths to each side of boot. Glue 1 end each of 3 holly leaves in a cluster to each side of boot above heel. Glue 1 heart over ends of each leaf cluster. Knot ends of hanger together to make a loop.

ROCKING HORSE

MATERIALS
- Patterns on page 137
- 12″ square of cream felt
- Felt scraps: tan, red
- Scrap of craft fleece
- 22″ (⅜″-wide) flat green trim
- 15″ (⅛″-wide) red grosgrain ribbon
- Craft glue
- Thread to match fabrics
- 2 (⅜″) green faceted plastic hearts
- 1 (⅛″) clear faceted plastic star

DIRECTIONS
1. Prepare materials. Transfer patterns and cut out as indicated. Trim edges of fleece body and fleece head ⅛″ smaller than patterns. Cut along short solid lines on tail and mane pieces for fringe. Cut green trim into 2 (4″) and 2 (5½″) lengths. Cut red ribbon into 1 (12″), 1 (1¼″), and 1 (1¾″) lengths.

2. Assemble body. Glue unfringed ends of tail pieces together. Glue tail to wrong side of 1 body piece. For hanger, fold 12″ length of ribbon in half and glue fold to wrong side of same body piece as indicated on pattern. With raw edges aligned, stack body piece with tail and hanger (right side down), fleece, and remaining body piece. With matching thread, whipstitch edges of body together, catching hanger in stitching. Glue 1 (5½″) length of green trim along top edge of rocker on each side of ornament. Referring to photo, glue 1 (4″) length of green trim around edge of each saddle piece. Glue 1 saddle piece to each side of body. With matching thread, whipstitch top edges of saddle together. Knot ends of hanger together to make a loop.

3. Assemble head. Stack 1 head piece, fleece, and remaining head piece. With matching thread, whipstitch around edges of head, leaving open as indicated on pattern. Insert neck in head opening and glue head to body. For bridle, glue 1¾″ and 1¼″ ribbon lengths across front

of head as indicated on pattern. Glue 1 mane piece to front and 1 to back of head. Referring to photo for placement, glue hearts to head for eyes and star to bridle on front of ornament.

COWBOY HAT

MATERIALS
- Patterns on page 138
- 2 (5″) squares of gold felt
- Felt scraps: red, green
- Scrap of craft fleece
- 24″ (⅛″-wide) green grosgrain ribbon
- Craft glue
- Gold thread
- 1 (⅜″) red faceted plastic heart

DIRECTIONS
1. Prepare materials. Transfer patterns and cut out as indicated. Trim edges of fleece hat piece ⅛″ smaller than pattern. Cut ribbon into 1 (12″) length and 4 (3″) lengths.

2. Assemble hat. For hanger, fold 12″ length of ribbon in half and glue fold to wrong side of 1 hat piece as indicated on pattern. With raw edges aligned, stack hat piece with hanger (right side down), fleece, and remaining hat piece. With matching thread, whipstitch edges of hat together, catching hanger in stitching.

3. Embellish hat. Glue 1 hatband 1″ above bottom edge on each side of hat. Referring to photo, glue 1 (3″) ribbon length to top and 1 to bottom of hatband on both sides of ornament. Glue holly leaves in a cluster to 1 side of hat. Glue heart over ends of leaves. Knot ends of hanger together to make a loop.

ANTIQUE HEARTS

MATERIALS FOR EACH:
- Pattern on page 138
- 1 (5" x 8") piece of lightweight cardboard
- Scrap of craft fleece
- Craft glue

For green heart:
- Scrap of light green moiré taffeta
- Thread to match taffeta
- Seed beads: gold, lavender
- Beading needle
- Assorted antique jewelry, buttons, and trims
- Embroidery floss: 3 coordinating colors

For red heart:
- Scrap of dark red moiré-patterned velvet
- Thread to match velvet
- ½ yard (⅛"-wide) olive rayon braid

DIRECTIONS

1. Prepare materials. For each: Transfer heart pattern to cardboard and fleece and cut 2 from each. Transfer heart pattern to fabric, add ½" seam allowance to all edges, and cut 2.

2. Make heart. For each: With matching thread, run a gathering thread around edge of each fabric heart. Aligning raw edges, stack 1 fleece heart on 1 cardboard heart; center, fleece side down, on wrong side of 1 fabric heart. Run a line of glue ¼" from edge around cardboard heart. Pull thread slightly to fit heart around cardboard and secure. Clip curves and press fabric edges to glue. Repeat with remaining fabric and cardboard hearts. With wrong sides facing, glue hearts together. **For green heart:** Referring to photo, embellish front of heart by sewing seed beads and gluing antique jewelry, buttons, and trims as desired. If desired, using 2 strands of floss, embroider buttonhole stitches through fabric only around edges of heart front.

3. Make hanger. For green heart: Cut 2 (9") lengths of each color of embroidery floss. Divide lengths into 2 stacks. Knot ends of 1 stack together 1" from 1 end. Braid floss to within 2" of opposite end. Repeat with remaining stack. Glue knots to opposite sides at top back of heart. Tie unbraided ends of floss together to make a loop. **For red heart:** Cut 2 (9") pieces of olive braid. Knot end of each braid 1" from 1 end. Glue knots to opposite sides at top back of heart. Tie lengths together 2" from ends to make a loop and fray ends.

How about an antique heart bellpull for Valentine's Day? Make five hearts minus their hangers and glue the backs of each to a length of grosgrain ribbon, doubled for strength.

KNITTED ANGEL

MATERIALS

- Phildar Sunset yarn: 1 ball gold
- DMC Tapestry Wool (8-yd. skein): 3 skeins white, 1 skein flesh (#7191)
- Scrap of black yarn
- 4 (size 1) double-pointed knitting needles
- Stuffing
- 1 package of brown crepe hair
- Hot-glue gun and glue stick
- ¾ yard (⅛″-wide) gold metallic braid
- ½ yard of prestrung pearl seed beads
- Thread: gold metallic, white
- 1 (500-count) package of pearl seed beads
- 30 (¼″-long) gold rice beads
- 1 (500-count) package of gold seed beads
- 9″ (2¾″-wide) white scalloped-edge lace with both scalloped edges finished

DIRECTIONS

Note: Carry yarn not in use behind work. Twist yarns when changing colors to prevent holes. Knitting abbreviations are on page 160.

1. Knit angel. Gauge: 6 sts = 1″, 8 rows = 1″. With gold, cast 40 sts onto 3 needles. *Rnd 1:* K around. *Rnd 2:* P around. *Rnds 3–4:* Rep rnds 1–2. *Rnds 5–6:* Join white, k 3, pick up gold, p 1, with white k 3, continue around as est. Cut yarn after rnd 6. *Rnds 7–35:* With white k around. Cut yarn after rnd 35. *Rnds 36–50:* Join flesh, k around. *Rnd 51:* (K 1, k 2 tog) around = 27 sts. *Rnd 52:* (K 2 tog, k 1) around = 18 sts. *Rnd 53:* Rep rnd 51 = 12 sts. *Rnd 54:* Rep rnd 52 = 8 sts. *Rnd 55:* Rep rnd 51 = 5 sts. Bind off, leaving a 6″ tail. Thread tail through remaining sts. Pull up tightly and secure. Weave in yarn ends.

2. Make ornament. Stuff ornament firmly. With gold yarn, slipstitch opening closed. To define head, sew a running stitch around neck (rnd 36) with flesh yarn, weaving over and under knit stitches. Pull tightly and secure. To define arm, with white yarn, begin about ½″ in from edge and stitch through ornament from neck down for 1½″, pulling stitches tightly. Repeat for other arm. Referring to photo for placement, make French knots with black yarn for eyes. Separate crepe hair and glue to head in tight curls.

3. Embellish ornament. For halo, cut 3 (9″) lengths of metallic braid. Braid the 3 lengths of metallic braid, wrap prestrung pearls around braid, and tack around angel's head with gold thread. Referring to Diagram, string pearl seed beads and gold rice beads and attach to body. To make wings, with white thread, stitch ends of lace together. Align the scallops and center the seam. With white thread, run a gathering thread along horizontal center through both layers of lace. Gather slightly to shape ends of wings and secure thread. With white thread, attach gold seed beads to edges of lace on both sides, following lace pattern. Run a gathering thread along vertical center through both layers of lace. Gather tightly and secure thread. Tack wings to center back of ornament. String gold seed beads to make 5 rows the length of the center of the wings and tack over gathered center. For hanger, sew an 8″ piece of metallic thread through top of angel and knot ends together to make a loop.

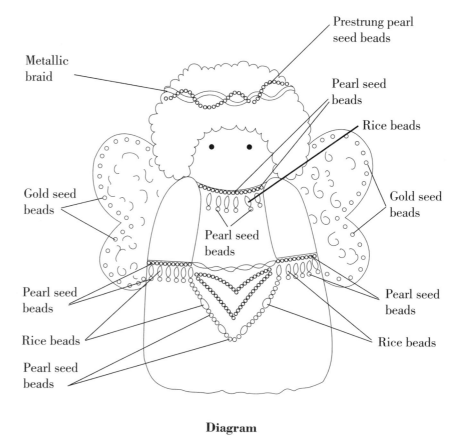

Metallic braid

Prestrung pearl seed beads

Pearl seed beads

Rice beads

Gold seed beads

Gold seed beads

Pearl seed beads

Pearl seed beads

Pearl seed beads

Rice beads

Rice beads

Pearl seed beads

Diagram

KNITTED SOLDIERS

BLUE JACKET SOLDIER

MATERIALS

- Patterns on page 138
- DMC Tapestry Wool (8-yd. skein): 1 skein each black, blue (#7319), red (#7666), flesh (#7121)
- 4 (size 1) double-pointed knitting needles
- Stuffing
- 1 package of brown crepe hair
- Hot-glue gun and glue sticks
- 9″ square of black satin
- Thread: black, gold metallic
- Scraps of assorted gold metallic trim
- 2″ gold metallic-thread tassel
- 4 (⅛″) gold beads
- 6 (⅛″) black beads

DIRECTIONS

Patterns include ¼″ seam allowance. *Note:* Knitting abbreviations are on page 160.

1. Knit soldier. Gauge: 6 sts = 1″, 8 rnds = 1″. With black, cast 40 sts onto 3 needles. *Rnds 1–4:* P around. *Rnds 5–12:* K around. Cut yarn after rnd 12. *Rnds 13–20:* With red, k around. Cut yarn after rnd 20. *Rnds 21–35:* With blue, k around. Cut yarn after rnd 35. *Rnds 36–50:* With flesh, k around. *Rnd 51:* (K 1, k 2 tog) around = 27 sts. *Rnd 52:* (K 2 tog, k 1) around = 18 sts. *Rnds 53–55:* Rep rnd 51. Bind off after rnd 55, leaving a 6″ tail. Thread tail through remaining sts. Pull up tightly and secure. Weave in yarn ends.

2. Make ornament. Stuff ornament firmly. With black yarn, slipstitch opening closed. To define head, sew a running stitch around neck (rnd 36) with flesh yarn, weaving over and under knit stitches. Pull tightly and secure. To define arm, with blue

yarn, begin about ½″ in from edge and stitch through ornament from neck to jacket bottom, pulling stitches tightly. Repeat for other arm. To define legs, with black yarn, stitch in same manner from center bottom to just above center top of boots. Referring to photo for placement, make French knots with black yarn for eyes. Separate crepe hair and glue to head in tight curls.

3. Make hat. Transfer and cut out hat top and hat brim patterns as indicated. Cut 2 (7½″ x 2¼″) strips from black satin for band. With right sides facing and raw edges aligned, stitch brim pieces together around curved edge, leaving straight edge open. Clip and turn. With right sides facing and raw edges aligned, stitch short ends of 1 strip together. Turn. Repeat with remaining strip, leaving wrong side out. With right sides facing, place 1 band inside the other, matching seams. Pin. Mark center of band opposite seam. Mark center of straight edge of brim. With raw edges aligned and center marks matching, slide brim between bands. Stitch around bottom edge of band, catching brim in seam. Turn. With right sides facing and raw edges aligned, stitch hat top to top edge of band. Referring to photo, glue scrap of gold trim around bottom edge of hat above brim. Tack tassel to top front. Stuff hat firmly. Glue hat on head.

4. Embellish ornament. Referring to photo, glue scraps of gold trim to ornament as shown. Tack 4 gold beads down center front of jacket. Tack 3 black beads to front of each boot. For hanger, sew an 8″ piece of metallic thread through top of hat and knot ends together to make a loop.

RED JACKET SOLDIER

MATERIALS

- Patterns on page 138
- DMC Tapestry Wool (8-yd. skein): 1 skein each black, white, red (#7666), flesh (#7121)
- 4 (size 1) double-pointed knitting needles
- Stuffing
- 1 package of brown crepe hair
- Hot-glue gun and glue sticks
- 9″ square of black satin
- Thread: black, gold metallic
- 2″ gold metallic-thread tassel
- Scraps of assorted gold metallic trim
- 6 (⅛″) gold beads

DIRECTIONS

Patterns include ¼″ seam allowance. *Note:* Knitting abbreviations are on page 160.

1. Knit soldier. Complete knitting instructions for soldier with blue jacket, substituting white for red in rnds 13–20 and red for blue in rnds 21–35.

2. Make ornament. Following steps 2 and 3 for blue soldier, complete ornament.

3. Embellish ornament. Referring to photo, cut 3 (1¼″) lengths of gold trim and glue lengths ¼″ apart on front of jacket. Tack 1 gold bead to each end of trim. Glue scraps of gold trim to front and back for belt. For hanger, sew an 8″ piece of metallic thread through top of hat and knot ends together to make a loop.

RIBBON DOVE AND HEART

DOVE

MATERIALS
- Pattern on page 139
- 2¼ yards (⅜"-wide) teal satin ribbon
- 2 (6") squares of teal fabric
- 6" square of paper-backed fusible web
- Thread to match teal ribbon
- Teal pearl cotton thread
- Polyester stuffing
- ¾ yard (⅛"-wide) lavender satin ribbon
- 2 (2") lengths of ⅜"-wide green satin ribbon
- 4" (½"-wide) yellow satin ribbon

DIRECTIONS
Pattern includes ¼" seam allowance.

1. Prepare materials. Cut teal ribbon into 6" pieces. Following manufacturer's instructions, fuse web to right side of 1 (6") square of teal fabric. With long edges abutting, pin ribbon lengths on web. Fuse ribbon to fabric. Transfer pattern to fused fabric and cut 1. Machine-zigzag raw edges. Transfer pattern to remaining 6" square and cut 1 for back.

2. Complete ornament. With pearl cotton, make small vertical stitches ½" apart between ribbon rows, catching edges of abutting ribbons in each stitch. With right sides facing and raw edges aligned, stitch dove front to back, leaving a 2" opening along bottom edge. Turn. Stuff firmly and slipstitch opening closed. Tie lavender ribbon in a bow around dove's neck. To make leaf, place 1 (2") green ribbon length wrong side up on flat surface. Fold left, then right, sides forward to form point at top (see Diagram A). Run a gathering thread across ribbon as shown; gather tightly and secure thread (see Diagram B). Trim any excess ribbon. Repeat with remaining green ribbon length. To make flower, place yellow ribbon wrong side up on flat surface. Fold both ends of ribbon at a right angle (see Diagram C). Run a gathering thread across bottom edge of ribbon, leaving needle and thread attached. Slightly gather ribbon and simultaneously wrap it in a circle to make flower (see Diagram D). Force needle through lower edge of ribbon and secure thread. Trim any excess ribbon. Tack leaves and then flower over lavender bow.

HEART

MATERIALS
- Pattern on page 139
- 2 yards (⅜"-wide) lavender satin ribbon
- 2 (6") squares of lavender fabric
- 6" square of paper-backed fusible web
- Thread to match lavender ribbon
- Light blue pearl cotton thread
- Polyester stuffing
- ¾ yard (¼"-wide) teal satin ribbon
- 2 (2") lengths of ⅜"-wide green satin ribbon
- 4" (½"-wide) yellow satin ribbon

DIRECTIONS
Pattern includes ¼" seam allowance.

1. Prepare materials. Complete step 1 of dove ornament, substituting above materials and heart pattern.

2. Complete ornament. With pearl cotton, make small vertical stitches between ribbon rows as for dove ornament. With pearl cotton and referring to photo, cross-stitch across 3d and then 4th rows, making each stitch the width of ribbon and stitching from vertical stitch at top of ribbon row to vertical stitch at bottom. With right sides facing and raw edges aligned, stitch heart front to back, leaving a 2" opening along 1 side. Turn. Stuff firmly and slipstitch opening closed. Tie teal ribbon in a bow and tack to top of heart. Following instructions in step 2 for dove and using green and yellow satin ribbon, make 2 leaves and 1 flower. Tack leaves and then flower over bow.

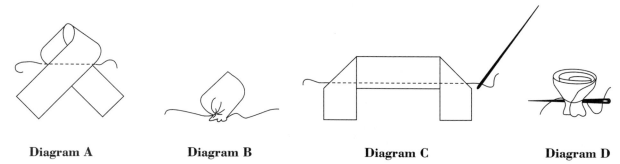

Diagram A   Diagram B   Diagram C   Diagram D

LEAF   FLOWER

SANTA AND SOLDIER NUTCRACKERS

MATERIALS (for 1)
- Patterns on page 139
- Completed cross-stitch design on white Aida 14
- Fabric scraps: **For Santa:** brown; **for soldier:** black, red
- Thread to match fabrics
- Stuffing
- Gold metallic thread

DIRECTIONS
Patterns include ¼″ seam allowance.

1. Prepare materials. For each: Cut out design piece, adding ¼″ seam allowance. **For Santa:** Transfer base pattern to brown fabric and cut 1. **For soldier:** Transfer base pattern to black fabric and cut 1. Transfer hat pattern to red fabric and cut 4.

2. Make ornament. For Santa: With right sides facing and raw edges aligned, fold design piece in half. Stitch back seam from bottom to top of hat. Stitch remaining edges of hat together to form a point. **For soldier:** With right sides facing and raw edges aligned, fold design piece in half. Stitch back seam. With right sides facing and raw edges aligned, stitch 2 hat pieces together along 1 side edge to make half of hat. Repeat with 2 remaining pieces. Stitch the 2 halves together. With right sides facing and raw edges aligned, stitch hat around top of soldier.

3. Complete ornament. For each: Turn ornament right side out and stuff firmly. Run a gathering thread around bottom edge of ornament and gather slightly. Turn under seam allowance around base piece and press. Slipstitch brown base to Santa and black base to soldier. For hanger, sew a 6″ piece of gold metallic thread through top of ornament and knot ends together to make a loop.

Give a copy of the classic The Nutcracker along with these handsome nutcracker ornaments and make this magical story come to life for a special child you know.

Stitch count: 72 x 82

SANTA

Stitched on white Aida 14 over 1 thread, the finished design size is 5⅛″ x 5⅞″. The fabric was cut 8″ x 8″.

Anchor			DMC (used for sample)
Step 1: Cross-stitch (2 strands)			
1	–		White
4146	·		754 Peach-lt.
8	I		761 Salmon-lt.
76	□		962 Wild Rose-med.
47	○		321 Christmas Red
20	✕		498 Christmas Red-dk.
131			798 Delft-dk.
942	○		738 Tan-vy. lt.
363	✕		436 Tan
378	–		841 Beige Brown-lt.
379	△		840 Beige Brown-med.
380	∴		839 Beige Brown-dk.
398	△		415 Pearl Gray
403	∴		310 Black

Step 2: Backstitch (1 strand)

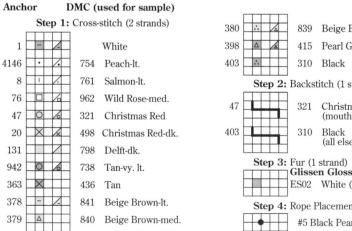

47		321 Christmas Red (mouth)
403		310 Black (all else)

Step 3: Fur (1 strand)
Glissen Gloss Estaz
ES02 White (2 cards)

Step 4: Rope Placement

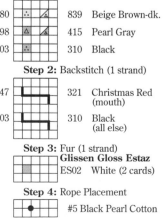

#5 Black Pearl Cotton

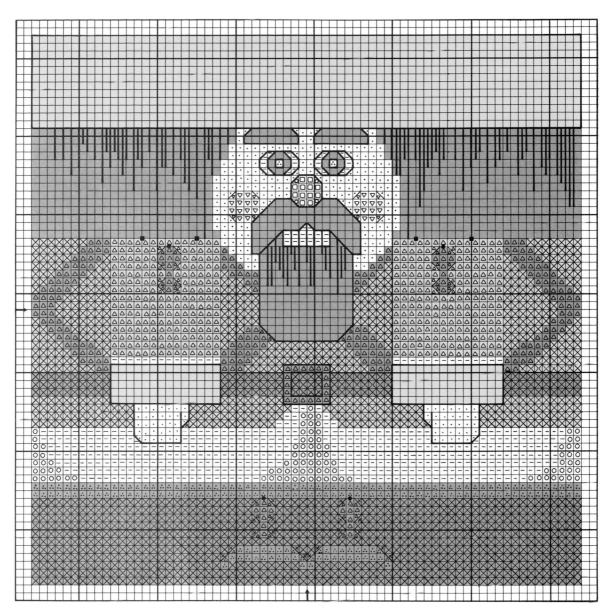

Stitch count: 70 x 70

SOLDIER

Stitched on white Aida 14 over 1 thread, the finished design size is 5″ x 5″. The fabric was cut 8″ x 8″.

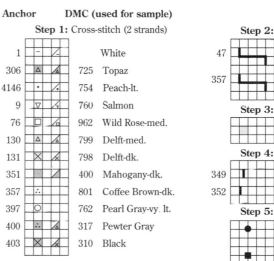

Anchor			DMC (used for sample)
Step 1: Cross-stitch (2 strands)			
1			White
306			725 Topaz
4146			754 Peach-lt.
9			760 Salmon
76			962 Wild Rose-med.
130			799 Delft-med.
131			798 Delft-dk.
351			400 Mahogany-dk.
357			801 Coffee Brown-dk.
397			762 Pearl Gray-vy. lt.
400			317 Pewter Gray
403			310 Black

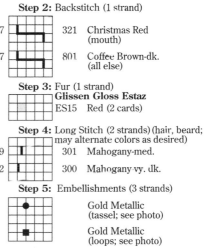

Step 2: Backstitch (1 strand)

47		321 Christmas Red (mouth)
357		801 Coffee Brown-dk. (all else)

Step 3: Fur (1 strand)
Glissen Gloss Estaz
ES15 Red (2 cards)

Step 4: Long Stitch (2 strands) (hair, beard; may alternate colors as desired)

349		301 Mahogany-med.
352		300 Mahogany vy. dk.

Step 5: Embellishments (3 strands)

Gold Metallic (tassel; see photo)

Gold Metallic (loops; see photo)

SOCK-COVERED ORNAMENTS

MATERIALS (for 2)
- 1 pair of child's white knee socks
- 2 (3″-diameter) craft foam balls
- ½ yard of pink fabric
- Thread to match sock
- 3 yards (¼″) cording
- Low-temperature glue gun and glue sticks

- 1½ yards (⅟₁₆″-wide) pink satin ribbon
- **For arch design:** embroidery floss: dark green, dark pink; 6 dark green diamond-faceted square stones
- **For spiral design:** pink embroidery floss, straight pins, 1½ yards prestrung 2-mm pearl beads

DIRECTIONS
1. **Prepare materials. For each:** Cut off and discard foot section of 1 sock. **For arch design:** Draw pencil line around vertical and horizontal centers of 1 craft foam ball. Divide each half into 3 equal vertical wedges and mark, for a total of 6 wedges. Mark parallel lines ⅛″ above and

50

below horizontal center mark. Referring to Diagram A and photo, mark 1 arch in upper half of each vertical wedge. Cut 2 (⅜″ x 20″) bias strips from pink fabric. **For spiral design:** Mark 6 equal horizontal sections on 1 craft foam ball, labeling top and bottom. Cut ⅜″-wide bias strips from pink fabric, piecing as needed to equal 1 (2½-yard) length. Cut pieced length into 1 (54″) and 2 (18″) lengths.

2. Make ornament. For arch design: Glue cording to craft foam ball along horizontal pencil lines and then all remaining lines, including arches (see Diagram A). Let dry. Slide ball inside center of sock. To cover cording and define ridges, using white thread, make small stitches back and forth under cording through all layers along all cording

designs (see Diagram B). Referring to photo, with 1 strand of green floss, straightstitch at ⅛″ intervals inside each arch in same manner. With 1 strand of pink floss, straightstitch between cording ridges at ⅛″ intervals around center of ornament (see Diagram B). Leaving 3″ tails at beginning and end, weave 1 bias strip through every other straight-stitch around center on 1 half of ball, making small loops (see Diagram C). Repeat for other side. Tie ends together on each side and make a bow. **For spiral design:** Beginning ½″ from center top of ball and using marks as guides for placement (see Diagram D), glue cording around ball in a descending spiral. Slide ball inside center of sock. Starting at top of ball, couch 54″ bias strip over cording at ¼″ intervals with 2 strands of pink floss (see Diagram E). Secure

1 end of prestrung pearls around straight pin. Referring to photo, insert pin below cording at top of ornament and run pearls following cording down to bottom of ornament, pinning as needed. Pin to secure end of pearls to bottom of ornament.

3. Complete ornament. For each: Run a gathering thread through sock at top of ornament. Pull to gather tightly to fit; secure. Fold top raw edges of sock under ¼″. Slipstitch together. Repeat on bottom of ornament. **For arch design:** Glue stones in lower half of each vertical wedge (see Diagram C). **For spiral design:** Make a loose bow with each 18″-long fabric strip and tack to bottom of ornament. **For each:** For hanger, thread ribbon through top of ornament and knot ends together to make a loop.

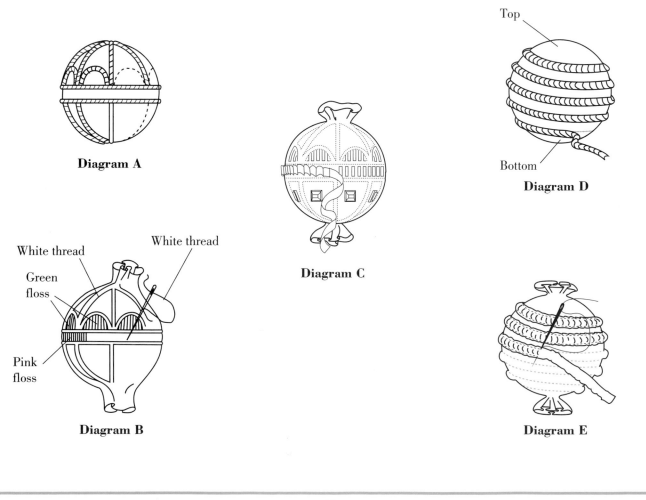

Diagram A

Diagram B

White thread   White thread

Green floss

Pink floss

Diagram C

Top

Bottom

Diagram D

Diagram E

PAINTED SANTA CONES

MATERIALS (for 1)
- Patterns on pages 139–140
- **For large Santa:** 8″ square of prepared canvas, 4″ square of foam-core board
- **For small Santa:** 6″ square of prepared canvas, 3″ square of foam-core board
- Acrylic paints: red, green, tan, white, black
- Paintbrushes
- Hot-glue gun and glue sticks
- 2 to 3 cups of unpopped popcorn

DIRECTIONS

1. Prepare materials. Transfer patterns for body and hat as indicated, including all details; do not cut out. Transfer pattern for base and cut out as indicated.

2. Paint ornament. Mix acrylic paints to obtain indicated colors and paint body and hat as directed on patterns. Using black paint and a thin paintbrush, add facial details, buttons, buckle, trim on sleeves and hat, and string on bag. Let dry. Cut out each piece.

3. Assemble Santa. Referring to pattern and photo, wrap body into a cone shape and glue along overlap line. Let dry. Wrap and glue hat to body. Let dry. Turn cone upside down and fill with popcorn to within ½″ of bottom edge. Place foam-core base over popcorn in bottom of body. Fold edges of body over foam core, clipping as needed, and glue. Glue canvas base to bottom of body.

JOLLY JESTERS

MATERIALS (for 1)
- Patterns on page 141
- 1 small package of Sculpey III in color for head, hands, and feet
- 1 small package of Sculpey III in contrasting color for details
- Craft glue
- ¼ yard of fabric
- ¼ yard of contrasting fabric
- Thread to match fabrics
- 1 (⅛″) gold jingle bell
- Stuffing
- ¼ yard (1″-wide) ribbon for collar
- 1 small novelty button
- 6″ (1/16″-wide) ribbon for hanger

DIRECTIONS
Patterns include ¼″ seam allowance.

1. Make body pieces. Following Diagram A, mold head, hands, and feet from Sculpey. Flatten ends of parts that will extend into clothing. Make cheeks, lips, and desired embellishments from contrasting Sculpey. Glue cheeks and lips to face and glue other details to hands or feet as desired. Using a straight pin and referring to photo, make slight indentations for eyes, nostrils, and eyebrows. Following manufacturer's instructions, bake or harden body pieces.

2. Make clothing. Transfer patterns to fabric and cut out. With right sides facing and raw edges aligned, sew body pieces together along A edges only. To make legs, fold body piece along broken line with right sides facing and raw edges aligned. Match B edges of each fabric piece to itself and sew together for inseam, pivoting at crotch. Turn. Fold end of 1 leg under ¼″ and run a gathering thread near fold; do not cut thread. Dot 1 flattened side of 1 foot with glue. Insert into 1 fabric leg, pull to gather thread around foot, and secure. Repeat with remaining leg and foot. With right sides facing, sew short edges of 1 sleeve piece together. Turn. Repeat with other sleeve piece. Fold end of 1 sleeve under ¼″ and run a gathering thread near fold; do not cut thread. Dot 1 flattened side of

1 hand with glue. Insert hand into 1 sleeve, pull to gather thread around wrist, and secure. Repeat with remaining sleeve piece and hand. With right sides facing, fold hat piece in half and stitch long edges together. Turn. Tack jingle bell to tip of hat.

3. Assemble body. Stuff legs and body lightly. Referring to Diagram B, fold top edge on each side of body into a ½″-deep pleat. Slip raw end of 1 sleeve inside 1 fold and tack securely. Repeat for other sleeve. Dot 1 flattened side of neck with glue. Insert neck inside top opening. Let dry overnight.

4. Complete ornament. Run a gathering thread close to 1 edge of collar ribbon. Pull to gather and tie ribbon around neck. Fold raw edge of hat under ¼″; adjust to fit head and glue hat to head. Referring to photo, tack button to front of body. For hanger, knot ends of 1/16″-wide ribbon together and tack knot at center back of body.

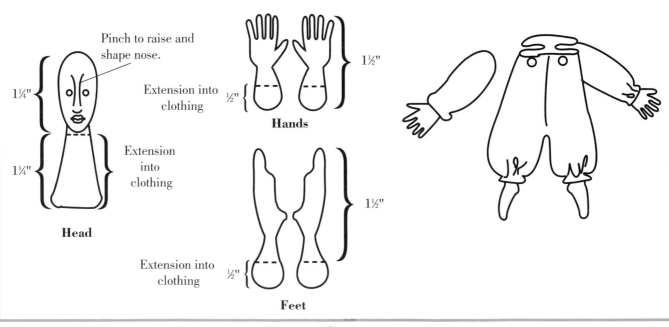

Diagram A

Pinch to raise and shape nose.

1¼″ Head

Extension into clothing

1¼″ Extension into clothing

1½″ Hands

½″ Extension into clothing

1½″ Feet

½″ Extension into clothing

Diagram B

YOUNG AT HEART

Christmas has always been a time for both the young and the young at heart, so enjoy! The happy woodland ornaments pictured here—simple cutouts with charming painted detail—are today's toys and tomorrow's folk art treasures. Like them, all the projects in this chapter evoke a spirit of holiday playfulness. Tuck a shiny frog prince in the branches of your tree. Add a painted canvas circus animal to a wrapped gift for a special present. Strike a musical note in your decorating with a snappy army band.

WOODLAND ORNAMENTS

MATERIALS (for 1)
- Patterns on pages 141–142
- 6″ square of ½″ pine
- Scroll saw
- Drill and ⅛″ bit
- Sandpaper
- Acrylic paints: see patterns
- Paintbrushes
- Hot-glue gun and glue stick
- Assorted trims: **For rabbit:** 3 (¼″) black ball buttons; **for ram:** 14 (¼″) pink heart beads; **for bird:** 11″ (1/16″) blue satin cord; **for tree:** 6″ (⅛″-wide) blue satin ribbon, 1 (½″-wide) unfinished wooden bead; **for squirrel:** 24 (¼″-wide) purple plastic flowers
- 9″ (⅛″-wide) blue satin ribbon for hanger

DIRECTIONS
1. Prepare materials. Transfer desired pattern to pine and, using scroll saw, cut out. For hanger, using ⅛″ bit, drill hole through top of ornament as indicated on pattern. Sand thoroughly. **For tree:** Using ⅛″ bit, drill hole through from 1 side to the other as indicated on pattern.

2. Paint and embellish ornament. For rabbit: Paint front and back with white base coat; let dry. Referring to pattern, finish painting. Let dry. Referring to photo, glue ball buttons on front. **For ram:** Paint front and back with rosy tan base coat; let dry. Referring to pattern, finish painting. Let dry. Referring to photo, glue beads on front and back. **For bird:** Paint front and back with light blue base coat; let dry. Referring to pattern, finish painting. Let dry. Tie cord in a bow around neck. **For tree:** Paint front and back with green base coat; let dry. Referring to pattern, finish

painting. Let dry. Thread 6″ ribbon through hole from side to side; then thread bead and knot ribbon ends together, placing knot inside hole. **For squirrel:** Paint front and back with medium brown base coat; let dry. Referring to pattern, finish painting. Let dry. Glue flowers on front and back. **For snowman:** Paint front and back with light blue base coat; let dry. Referring to pattern, finish painting. Let dry.

3. Make hanger. For tree: Thread 9″ ribbon under ribbon at top and knot ends together to make a loop. **For all others:** Thread 9″ ribbon through hole in top of ornament and knot ends together to make a loop.

LIME VICKY

MATERIALS
- Chenille pipe cleaners
- Assorted large and small sequins
- 6 diamond-faceted glass beads
- Straight pins
- 1 large lime
- 1 (⅜") button
- Paring knife
- Yarn scraps: yellow, red
- 1 popsicle stick
- Nylon thread
- Long needle

DIRECTIONS

1. Make face. Cut pipe cleaners into 2 (4") and 2 (5") lengths. For each eye, thread 1 large sequin, 1 glass bead, and 1 small sequin onto 1 straight pin and stick into lime. For nose, pin button to face. For mouth, pin 3 large sequins to face. To make eyebrows, use paring knife to poke 2 holes 1" apart above 1 eye. Insert ends of 1 (4") pipe cleaner into holes above eye, shaping as desired (see photo). Repeat for other eyebrow.

2. Attach hair and earrings. For hair, cut 12 (5") lengths from yellow yarn and 10 (5") lengths from red yarn. Hold all yarn lengths together and knot another yarn length around center of bunch. Refer to photo for placement and pin hair through knot to lime. To make earrings, use paring knife to poke 1 hole on each side of face. Thread 1 (5") pipe cleaner through 2 beads. Fold pipe cleaner in half and twist ends together. Insert twisted ends in hole on 1 side of face. Repeat for other earring.

3. Complete ornament. Using paring knife, make a slit the width of popsicle stick in bottom of ornament. Insert half of popsicle stick into slit. For hanger, sew a piece of nylon thread through top of ornament and knot ends together to make a loop.

FROG PRINCES

MATERIALS (for 1)
- Patterns on page 143
- ¼ yard of green lamé
- 5″ square of gold lamé
- ¼ yard of lightweight fusible interfacing
- Thread: green, gold
- 2 cups of uncooked rice for stuffing
- 3½″ (¾″-wide) gold metallic lace trim
- Monofilament

DIRECTIONS
Patterns include ¼″ seam allowance.

1. Prepare materials. Transfer patterns and cut out as indicated. Following manufacturer's instructions, fuse interfacing to wrong side of body pieces.

2. Construct frog. With right sides facing and raw edges aligned, stitch 2 front leg pieces together, leaving open as indicated on pattern. Clip curves and turn. Repeat for remaining legs. Stitch dart in both body pieces as indicated on pattern. Referring to pattern for placement and aligning ends of legs with raw edges of body, stitch legs to right side of green body piece. Fold legs to middle of right side of body and pin. With right sides facing and raw edges aligned, stitch body pieces together, leaving an opening at dart. Turn. Fill legs moderately with rice and slipstitch openings closed. Repeat for body.

3. Complete ornament. To make crown, fold gold trim in half, overlapping ends slightly, and whipstitch ends together. Tack to head. For hanger, sew a piece of monofilament through top of ornament and knot ends together to make a loop.

Made of corduroy or some other durable fabric, these frog princes would jump for joy as beanbag toys—perfect as last-minute gifts for both girls and boys.

PAINTED CIRCUS ANIMALS

MATERIALS (for 1)
- Patterns on pages 143–144
- Dressmaker's pen
- Scrap of white 25-count Lugana cross-stitch fabric
- Thread to match
- Scrap of white canvas for base
- Stuffing
- Scrap of foam-core board
- Hot-glue gun and glue sticks
- Acrylic paints: see patterns
- Assorted paintbrushes
- ½ yard (⅞"-wide) cream satin ribbon
- **For lion:** 2 yards (⅛"-wide) olive grosgrain ribbon, thread to match
- **For elephant:** ¾ yard (¹⁄₁₆") light blue satin cording
- **For zebra:** Scraps of blue paper cording

DIRECTIONS
Patterns include ¼" seam allowance.

1. Prepare materials. For each:
Using dressmaker's pen, transfer patterns and markings for desired animal and base and cut out as indicated.

2. Make animal. For elephant:
With right sides facing, raw edges aligned, and using ¼" seams, stitch 2 ears together, leaving open as indicated on pattern. Clip seam allowance and turn. Repeat for other ear. Referring to pattern for placement, satin-stitch 1 ear to each elephant piece. **For each:** With wrong sides facing, raw edges aligned, and using a narrow zigzag, machine-satin-stitch edges of animal together, leaving bottom edge open. Trim close to satin stitching and satin-stitch again over first stitching. Stuff animal firmly to within ½" of bottom edge (but do not stuff elephant's trunk). Insert foam-core base. Fold bottom edges of Lugana over foam core and glue. Glue canvas base to foam-core base.

3. Paint animal. For each:
Referring to pattern and photo, paint both sides of animal as desired. Let dry.

4. Complete animal. For lion:
Referring to photo, make 1" loops with grosgrain ribbon and tack to head for mane. **For elephant:** With white thread, stitch back and forth through all layers under body of elephant between stirrup and hind leg, pulling thread tightly to define body. Beginning and ending at back of neck, couch a 16" piece of blue cording with white thread around saddle. Wrap a 16" piece of cording around neck and tie in a bow at back of neck. **For zebra:** For mane, cut paper cording into ¾" pieces. Referring to photo, glue pieces to each side at back of neck and top of head. **For each:** Tie satin ribbon in a bow around neck.

63

ARMY BAND

MATERIALS (for 1)
- Patterns on page 145
- ¼ yard of olive green wool
- Wool scraps: pink, black
- Liquid ravel preventer
- Thread: pink, olive green, black
- Stuffing
- 13″ (¼″-wide) red-and-green flat trim
- Fabric glue
- 2 (2½″) lengths of gold fringe
- 2 (2½″) lengths of ⅜″-wide wavy gold braid
- 5″ (¼″-wide) flat gold trim
- 1 spool of gold metallic thread
- 10 (2-mm) gold beads
- 6 (2-mm) black beads
- 4½″ (1⁄16″-wide) black rayon braid
- 1 (1″) purchased gold tassel
- 1 (10″) length of red cording
- 1 gold-colored ornament: 1½″-diameter drum or 3″-long horn

DIRECTIONS
Patterns include ¼″ seam allowance where needed.

1. Prepare materials. Transfer patterns and cut out as indicated. Apply liquid ravel preventer to raw edges of all wool pieces.

2. Make body. With raw edges aligned, sew face pieces together, leaving top open. Turn. Topstitch face to head of 1 body piece as indicated on pattern. With right sides facing and raw edges aligned, sew body pieces together, leaving open as indicated on pattern. Turn and clip seam allowance as needed in neck and inseam. Stuff firmly and slip-stitch opening closed. Cut 2 (4″) lengths of red-and-green trim. Glue 1 trim length over side seam of each leg. With raw edges aligned, sew 2 boot pieces together. Clip and turn. Stuff firmly to within ½″ of top edge. Fold top edge of boot ¼″ to inside. With boot seam centered at front and back of leg, insert 1 leg in boot and slipstitch boot to leg. Repeat for other boot.

3. Make arms and hands. With raw edges aligned, sew 2 hand pieces together with ⅛″ seam, leaving open as indicated on pattern. Do not turn. Stuff hand lightly. Repeat for other hand. With raw edges aligned, fold 1 arm piece in half lengthwise and sew long edges together. Turn. Slipstitch top edge closed. Stuff arm firmly. Apply glue to wrist edge of 1 hand and insert hand in arm. Let dry. Stitch through all layers of arm at elbow to make joint. Repeat for other arm. Stitch tops of arms to body at shoulders. Glue 2 epaulets together and then glue whole epaulet to 1 shoulder, covering top of arm. Let dry. Repeat for other epaulet.

4. Add clothing. Glue waist edge of peplum/tails piece around waist of body, overlapping short edges at center front. With collar standing up, glue shorter edge of collar around neck, overlapping ends at center front. Roll collar down. Glue straight edge of hat bill over top edge of face.

5. Complete ornament. Referring to photo, glue 1 fringe length along top edge of each epaulet, trimming fringe width to ⅜″. Glue wavy gold braid over top of fringe. Cut 2 (2½″) lengths of red-and-green trim and glue 1 length around each arm, ¼″ above wrist. Glue 5″ length of ¼″-wide flat gold trim around waist. Cut 1 (4″) and 3 (3″) pieces of gold metallic thread. Fold 4″ piece in quarters. Flatten to look like braid and glue across top of tails between Xs (see pattern). Glue 1 gold bead to each end of thread. Fold 3″ pieces in quarters. Flatten to look like braid and glue ¼″ apart on center front of body (see photo). Glue gold beads to ends of each piece. Sew 3 black beads ¼″ apart to center front of each boot. Glue black braid across top of hat bill; then drape and glue braid around edge of face, meeting first end. Trim and glue. Glue 1 gold bead to each corner of bill. Tack tassel to center top of hat. Tie red cording to instrument ornament, leaving a 1½″ tail on each end; fringe ends. Slip cord around neck of soldier (see photo). For hanger, sew a 6″ piece of gold metallic thread through top of head and knot ends together to make a loop.

MATERIALS
- Worsted-weight acrylic (110-yd. ball): 1 each burgundy, dark green
- Size E crochet hook (or size to obtain gauge)
- ¾ yard (⅛"-wide) burgundy satin ribbon (optional)

DIRECTIONS
Gauge: 5 sc and 5 rows = 1". *Note:* Crochet abbreviations are on page 160.

1. Crochet mittens. Make 2. **Wrist:** With burgundy, ch 30, join with a sl st to form a ring. *Rnds 1–3:* Ch 1, sc in ea st around, sl st in beg ch. (*Note:* Use a safety pin to mark the beg of ea rnd. Work in bk lps only in a spiral.) *Rnd 4:* Sc in ea st around. *Rnd 5:* Work 2 sc in first st, sc in next st, 2 sc in next st, sc in ea rem st around. *Rnd 6:* Sc in ea st around. *Rnd 7:* Work 2 sc in first st, sc in ea of next 3 sts, 2 sc in next st, sc in ea rem st around. *Rnds 8–9:* Sc in ea st around. *Rnd 10:* Sc in ea of next 10 sts, ch 2, join with a sl st in first sc of rnd for thumb. Do not fasten off. **Thumb:** *Rnd 1:* Working in bk lps only in a spiral as est, sc in ea sc and ch around. *Rnds 2–7:* Sc in ea st around. *Rnd 8:* * Pull up a lp in ea of next 2 sts, yo and through all lps (dec over 2 sts made), rep from * around to last 4 sts. Fasten off, leaving a 6" tail. Thread tail through bk lps of rem 4 sts, pull tightly, and secure. **Hand:** *Rnd 1:* Working in bk lps only in a spiral as est, join burgundy with sc in first ch of thumb ch-2, sc in next ch and ea st around. *Rnds 2–10:* Sc in ea st around. (Dec over next 2 sts) around until only 6 sts rem. Fasten off, leaving a 6" tail. Thread tail through bk lps of rem sts, pull tightly, and secure. **Trim:** *Rnd 1:* Join burgundy in first ch of wrist near thumb, ch 4 for first dc and ch 1, * sk 1 st, dc in next st, ch 1, rep from * around, sl st in 3rd ch of beg ch-4. *Rnd 2:* Ch 1, sc in ea dc and sp around, sl st in beg ch. Fasten off. **Loops:** *Rnd 1:* With wrong side facing, join dark green in first st of prev rnd, ch 1, make lp st as foll: * wind yarn loosely around index finger of left hand 5 times, insert hook in next sc and through lps on finger, yo and pull through lps and sc, yo and pull through 2 lps on hook, pull st tight, sl lps off finger, sc in next st, rep from * around, sl st in beg ch. *Rnd 2:* Ch 1, sc in ea st around, sl st in beg ch. *Rnds 3–4:* Rep rnds 1–2. *Rnd 5:* Rep rnd 1. Fasten off.

2. Complete mittens. For each mitten, fold a 9" length of ribbon in half to make a loop. Tack ribbon ends inside mitten cuff for hanger.

3. Crochet stocking. Foot: *Row 1:* With burgundy, beg at heel, ch 16, sc in 2nd ch from hook and ea st across = 15 sts, ch 1, turn. *Rows 2–11:* Working in bk lps only, sc in ea st across, ch 1, turn. *Row 12:* Working in bk lps only, sc in ea st across, ch 1, turn, ch 8 for instep, join with a sl st in first st of row = 23 sts. (*Note:* Use a safety pin to mark the beg of ea rnd. Work in bk lps only in a spiral.) *Rnd 1:* Ch 1, sc in ea st around. *Rnd 2:* Sc in ea st around. *Rnd 3:* Pull up a lp in ea of next 2 sts, yo and through all lps (dec over 2 sts made), sc in ea of next 12 sts, dec over next 2 sts, sc in ea of next 7 sts = 21 sts. *Rnd 4:* Sc in ea st around. *Rnd 5:* Dec over next 2 sts, sc in ea of next 10 sts, dec over next 2 sts, sc in ea of next 7 sts = 19 sts. *Rnds 6–7:* * Dec over next 2 sts, sc in next st, rep from * around, sl st in next st = 8 sts rem after rnd 7.

Fasten off, leaving a 6" tail. Thread tail through bk lps of rem sts, pull tightly, and secure. **Instep:** *Row 1:* Join burgundy in first st of instep ch-8, sc in ea of next 8 ch, sl st in side of next st on foot, turn. *Row 2:* Sc in ea of next 8 sts, sl st in side of next st on foot, turn. *Row 3:* Sc in next st, dec over next 2 sts, sc in ea of next 2 sts, dec over next 2 sts, sc in last st, sl st in side of next st on foot = 6 sts. Fasten off. **Leg:** *Row 1:* Join burgundy at heel, working in side of foot rows, ch 1, sc in ea of 9 sts to instep, sc in ea of 6 sts across instep, sc in ea of 10 sts along other side of foot to heel = 26 sts, turn. *Row 2:* Working in ft lps only, ch 1, sc in ea st across, turn. *Row 3:* Ch 1, working in bk lps only, sc in ea st across, turn. *Row 4:* Rep row 2. *Row 5:* Rep row 3, do not turn. Join with a sl st in first st of row. *Rnd 1:* Working in bk lps only in a spiral as est, ch 1, 2 sc in next st, sc in ea st to 2 sts from end of rnd, 2 sc in next st, sc in last st = 28 sts. *Rnds 2–3:* Sc in ea st around. *Rnd 4:* Sc in next st, 2 sc in next st, sc in ea st to 2 sts from of rnd, 2 sc in next, sc in last st = 30 sts. *Rnds 5–6:* Sc in ea st around. *Rnd 7:* Rep rnd 4 = 32 sts. *Rnds 8–10:* Rep rnds 5–7 = 34 sts after rnd 10. *Rnd 11:* Sl st in next st, ch 4 for first dc and ch 1, * sk 1 st, dc in next st, ch 1, rep from * around, sl st in 3rd ch of beg ch. *Rnd 12:* Ch 1, sc in ea dc and sp around, sl st in beg ch. Fasten off. **Loops:** *Rnds 1–5:* Work as for mitten loops rnds 1–5.

4. Complete stocking. With burgundy, whipstitch heel seam. Fold a 9" length of ribbon or yarn in half to make a loop. Tack ribbon ends inside stocking cuff for hanger.

SWEET TREATS

BUBBLE GUM MACHINE

MATERIALS
- Patterns on page 146
- Felt scraps: gray, white, black, red, pink, green, yellow, light blue, dark blue
- Craft glue
- Scrap of fleece
- Thread: gray, white
- 12" (⅛"-wide) red grosgrain ribbon

DIRECTIONS
1. Prepare materials. Transfer patterns and cut out as indicated.

2. Assemble gum machine. On right side of 1 glass piece, glue 4 bubble gum balls along bottom edge. Repeat with other glass piece. With right sides up, glue 1 top and 1 bottom to 1 glass piece, slightly covering row of gum balls. Repeat with remaining top, bottom, and glass piece. Using 1 gum machine piece as pattern, cut 1 from fleece and trim fleece edges ⅛" all around. For hanger, fold ribbon in half and glue fold at top center on wrong side of 1 gum machine piece. Stack gum machine

piece with hanger (wrong side up), fleece, and other gum machine piece (right side up). With matching thread, whipstitch edges together, catching hanger in stitching. Knot ribbon ends together to make hanger loop.

3. Complete ornament. Glue slot back, slot front, and 1 gum ball to center back of machine (see Diagram). Glue numeral 5 and cent sign side by side to center front. Referring to photo, glue remaining gum balls to both sides of glass, slightly overlapping edges of balls.

ICE CREAM CONE

MATERIALS
- Patterns on page 146
- Felt scraps: tan, cream, brown, white, green, red
- 20" (⅛"-wide) brown grosgrain ribbon
- Dressmaker's pen
- Craft glue
- Scrap of fleece
- 12" (⅛"-wide) cream grosgrain ribbon
- Thread to match fabrics

DIRECTIONS
1. Prepare materials. Transfer patterns and cut out as indicated. Cut brown ribbon into 2 (2½"), 4 (1⅞"), 2 (1⅜"), 2 (1¼"), and 2 (¾") lengths.

2. Complete ornament. Referring to Diagram, mark placement for ribbon "lattice" on 1 side of each cone piece with dressmaker's pen. Glue ribbon to cone pieces, trimming ends even. Referring to Diagram and photo, glue bottom scoop on lattice side of each cone, overlapping ends of ribbons slightly as shown and aligning pieces on front and back. Repeat with remaining scoops. Using 1 cone piece as pattern, cut 1 piece from fleece and trim fleece edges ⅛" all around. Glue holly leaves and then cherries to top scoops. For hanger, fold cream ribbon in half and glue fold at top center on wrong side of 1 cone piece. Stack cone piece with hanger (wrong side up), fleece, and other cone piece (right side up). With matching thread, whipstitch edges together, catching hanger in stitching. Knot ribbon ends together to make hanger loop.

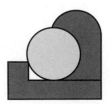

Diagram: Bubble Gum Machine

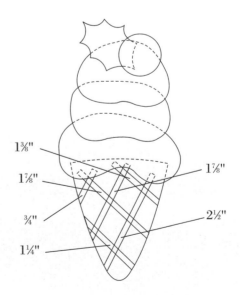

Diagram: Ice Cream Cone

HOLIDAY ROMANCE

Capture the romance of an old-fashioned Christmas with the array of elegant decorations in this chapter. The color of bronze refines the delicate twig wreaths and trees on these pages. Ornaments embroidered with satiny ribbon will add luxury to your tree, as will a paper angel touched with beautiful marbleizing. Fill your collection of antique saltshakers with potpourri and hang them next to opulent cross-stitched tapestry balls. And enjoy the sophisticated cachet of a plastic canvas jewel, whose geometric charms could grace your proudest present.

BRONZED TWIG ORNAMENTS

MATERIALS (for 1)
- Patterns on page 147
- 6" square of heavy textured fabric (such as burlap or Aida cloth)
- White glue
- Waxed paper
- Small twigs
- ½ yard (¼"-wide) silk ribbon
- Assorted trims: tiny artificial flowers, leaves, bird's nests, plastic birds, beads
- ⅜ yard (1-mm) prestrung beads (optional)
- ¼ yard of gold metallic thread
- Copper spray paint

DIRECTIONS

1. Prepare materials. Transfer desired pattern to fabric and cut 1. Dilute glue with water until it is the consistency of milk; soak fabric in glue and wrinkle as desired (see photo). Let fabric dry overnight on waxed paper.

2. Make ornament. Using undiluted glue, attach twigs to fabric as desired. Trim any twig ends that extend beyond edges of fabric. Make small bows from ribbon as desired; twist remaining ribbon length slightly and glue ribbon and bows to ornament. Add assorted trims as desired.

3. Complete ornament. For hanger, sew a 6″ piece of gold thread through top of ornament and knot ends together to make a loop. Spray entire ornament with copper spray paint. Let dry.

SALT 'N PEPPER SHAKERS

MATERIALS (for 1)
• Purchased new or antique individual-serving glass salt shaker
• Very fine potpourri, dried berries, rose petals, or cloves
• Gold or silver metallic thread to match shaker top
• 22″ (¹⁄₁₆″-wide) satin ribbon or braid
• Small amount of baby's breath

and/or assorted tiny dried flowers
• Craft glue

DIRECTIONS
1. Make ornament. Fill salt shaker as desired with potpourri, berries, rose petals, or cloves. For hanger, thread gold or silver metallic thread through 2 holes in shaker top and knot ends together to make a loop.

2. Embellish ornament. Cut ribbon in half; knot both lengths around neck of shaker. Handling both ribbons as 1, make a bow. Knot ribbon ends. Glue baby's breath and/or dried flowers around shaker top as desired.

MARBLEIZED PAPER ANGEL

MATERIALS
- Patterns on page 148
- Newspapers
- Disposable aluminum roasting pan
- Liquid starch
- Large plastic trash bag
- Acrylic paints in colors of choice
- Plastic cups (1 for each color of paint)
- Eyedroppers (1 for each color of paint)
- Wide-toothed comb
- 2 (6" x 8") sheets of white 2-ply smooth-finish Bristol board
- Tongs
- 1 small squeegee
- Waxed paper
- Scrap of watercolor paper
- Scrap of fleece
- Scrap of paisley fabric
- White thread
- Craft glue
- Artist's paintbrush

DIRECTIONS

1. Prepare marbleizing materials. Cut or tear 1 or 2 sections of newspaper into strips about 2" wide and as long as width of marbleizing pan. Spread remaining newspaper over work surface. Place pan on newspapers; pour in liquid starch to a depth of about 2". (Save starch bottle to use for storing and discarding used starch.) Cut trash bag open along 1 side and spread flat beside pan to make a waterproof surface for drying marbleized paper. Pour about 2 tablespoons of 1 color of acrylic paint into plastic cup. Thin paint with water to consistency of whole milk. Prepare other colors in same way. (Use 4 or fewer colors for any marbleizing project.)

2. Marbleize paper. Fill 1 eyedropper with paint. With eyedropper close to surface of starch, gently float several drops of paint. Paint should spread into a thin 3"- to 5"-diameter circle. (Some paint will sink to bottom, but this will not affect marbleizing process. If all paint sinks to bottom or stays in a glob on surface, paint is too thick; add several drops of water to paint, mix well, and, after skimming old paint from surface of starch with newspaper strips, try again.) Float additional colors on top of first color (colors will not mix) or in random pattern of adjacent circles. Apply paint until surface is covered. To create patterns, hold comb at a 90° angle to surface and carefully swirl or rake surface only. Holding 1 sheet of Bristol board over surface, gently lower it so that center contacts surface first. Gently lower rest of paper so that corners and edges come into contact last. Smooth paper from center outward to remove any air bubbles. Do not readjust or reposition paper. Allow to sit about 5 seconds; then lift paper at edge carefully with tongs, raking design surface along edge of pan to remove excess liquid. Place marbleized paper right side up on plastic bag and gently squeegee liquid off; place on waxed paper and let dry thoroughly. After marbleizing each paper, drag the newspaper strips across the pan to clean off leftover paint. Some paint will sink to the bottom, but this will not affect the next print. Repeat process for second piece of paper.

3. Prepare angel materials. Transfer patterns for body, face, and hands and cut out as indicated. Referring to pattern, cut 1 piece of fleece to match skirt; trim ½" from side and bottom edges. Cut 3 individual motifs from paisley fabric.

4. Assemble angel. Referring to pattern, cut slashes in angel wings for front only. With wrong sides of body pieces facing and referring to pattern, topstitch angel wings along broken lines through both layers with longest machine stitch. Add a drop of glue to ends of stitching to prevent raveling. Center fleece in skirt area between layers of paper. Glue edges of paper together around skirt and above head.

5. Complete ornament. Referring to pattern and photo, paint details on front of angel. On face, paint hair and facial features. Let dry. Glue face and hands to front of angel. Glue fabric motifs to skirt. For hanger, sew a 9" piece of thread through top of angel and knot ends together to make a loop.

JEWELED VELVET ORNAMENTS

MATERIALS FOR EACH:
- Patterns on pages 150–151
- Beading needle
- Stuffing
- Large-eyed needle
- Tailor's chalk

For heart:
- Scrap of burgundy velvet
- Thread to match fabric
- 3 (¾"-long) dark pink oval costume jewelry stones
- 1 package (³⁄₁₆"-long) clear bugle beads
- 1 package (³⁄₁₆"-long) blue bugle beads
- 1 package of pink seed beads
- ½ yard (⅝"-wide) burgundy braid
- 10" (¹⁄₁₆") burgundy cord

For diamond:
- Scrap of off-white velvet
- Thread to match fabric
- 1 (1") orange round costume jewelry stone
- 10 (¾"-long) green oval costume jewelry stones
- 8 (⅞"-long) clear teardrop costume jewelry stones

- 1 package (³⁄₁₆"-long) orange bugle beads
- 1 package (³⁄₁₆"-long) yellow bugle beads
- 1 package (³⁄₁₆"-long) green bugle beads
- 36 clear seed beads
- 24 orange seed beads
- 24 yellow seed beads
- 20" (⅝"-wide) white braid
- 10" (¹⁄₁₆") white cord

For shell:
- Scrap of navy velvet
- Thread to match fabric
- 5 (⅞"-long) pink teardrop costume jewelry stones
- 3 (⅞"-long) clear teardrop costume jewelry stones
- 1 package (³⁄₁₆"-long) green bugle beads
- 1 package (³⁄₁₆"-long) gold bugle beads
- 1 package (³⁄₁₆"-long) pink bugle beads
- 1 package (³⁄₁₆"-long) clear bugle beads
- 48 green seed beads
- 32 pink seed beads

- 20 clear seed beads
- ½ yard (⅛"-wide) gold braid
- 8" (⅛") gold cord

DIRECTIONS
Patterns include ¼" seam allowance.

1. Prepare materials. Transfer desired pattern to velvet and cut 2. Referring to pattern, mark placement for stones on right side of 1 velvet piece. Stitch stones and beads to velvet piece as indicated on pattern.

2. Make ornament. With straight edge of braid aligned with raw edge of fabric, stitch braid to right side of beaded ornament, overlapping ends. With right sides facing, stitch ornament pieces together along stitching line of braid, leaving open as indicated on pattern. Turn. Stuff firmly and slip-stitch opening closed. For hanger, sew cord through top of ornament and knot ends together to make a loop.

Leave off some of its beads and this lovely velvet heart ornament becomes a handy pin cushion. Wouldn't it make a thoughtful present for Mother's Day?

CROSS-STITCHED TAPESTRY BALL

MATERIALS (for 1)
- Completed cross-stitch designs on Silk Gauze 30
- 3″-diameter craft foam ball
- Small paring knife
- 14″ (½″-wide) burgundy flat braid
- Thread to match braid
- 70 gold seed beads
- Low-temperature glue gun and glue stick
- 1 (5″) purchased burgundy tassel
- ¼ yard of burgundy cording

DIRECTIONS

1. Prepare materials. Cut out design pieces, adding ¼″ seam allowance to each. Mark top center and bottom center of craft foam ball. Divide circumference of ball into 3 equal wedge-shaped sections and mark. Score ball along section lines, using paring knife.

2. Assemble ornament. Center 1 design piece over 1 section of ball. Using paring knife, poke fabric into ball along score lines, taking small tucks as needed to smooth fabric over surface. (Keep score lines as narrow and inconspicuous as possible.) Trim excess fabric close to ball. Repeat with remaining designs.

3. Embellish ornament. Sew gold seed beads ⅜″ apart along both long edges of braid. Glue beaded braid over score lines, overlapping and gluing ends to secure. Glue tassel to bottom of ornament. For hanger, knot ends of cording together to make a loop and glue to top of ornament.

Sample for Tapestry Ball
Stitched on Silk Gauze 30 over 2 threads, the finished design size is 2⅝″ x 4″. The fabric was cut 5″ x 6″. Stitch 3.

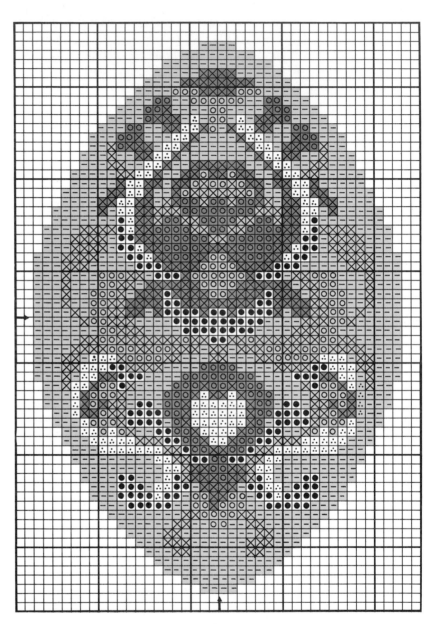

Stitch count: 40 x 60

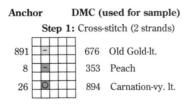

Anchor		DMC (used for sample)
	Step 1: Cross-stitch (2 strands)	
891	–	676 Old Gold-lt.
8	–	353 Peach
26	○	894 Carnation-vy. lt.

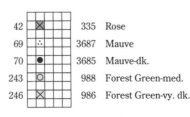

Anchor		DMC
42	✕	335 Rose
69	∴	3687 Mauve
70	●	3685 Mauve-dk.
243	○	988 Forest Green-med.
246	✕	986 Forest Green-vy. dk.

78

THREE-DIMENSIONAL ORNAMENTS

MATERIALS (for 1)
- Silver metallic yarn
- Large-eyed needle
- **For Ornament A:** Completed cross-stitch designs on 2 Plastic Canvas 7 (3″-diameter) circles, on 2 Plastic Canvas 14 squares, and on 1 Plastic Canvas 7 band
- **For Ornament B:** Completed cross-stitch designs on 1 Plastic Canvas 7 (4¼″ x 3⅛″) diamond
- **For Ornament C:** Completed cross-stitch designs on Plastic Canvas 14
- **For Ornament D:** Completed cross-stitch designs on Plastic Canvas 7

DIRECTIONS
Complete ornament. For Ornament A: Cut out each cross-stitched square and band 1 hole outside design. With 1 strand of silver metallic yarn, overcast-stitch 1 square

to center of each circle. Overcast-stitch edge of 1 circle to each long edge of band. Overcast-stitch ends of band together. For hanger, sew a 4½″ piece of metallic yarn through top of ornament and knot ends together to make a loop. **For Ornament B:** Cut out each cross-stitched diamond 1 hole outside design. With 1 strand of silver metallic yarn, overcast-stitch all sections together to form a diamond-shaped box. For hanger, sew a 2½″ piece of metallic yarn through top of ornament and knot ends together to make a loop. **For Ornament C:** Cut out each cross-stitched piece 1 hole outside design. With 1 strand of silver metallic yarn, overcast-stitch sides together to form a 4-sided piece. Fold down flaps of 1 cap and overcast-stitch sides of flaps together to form a square. Repeat for other cap. Place 1 cap on each end of 4-sided piece. Overcast-stitch to

4-sided piece. Tack at corners of caps to secure. For hanger, sew a 3¼″ piece of metallic yarn through top of ornament and knot ends together to make a loop. **For Ornament D:** Repeat directions for ornament C, alternating ruby Scotch-stitched sides with emerald Scotch-stitched sides and making hanger thread length 6½″.

Sample for Ornament A
Circle: Stitched on Plastic Canvas 7 (3″-diameter) circle over 1 mesh, the finished design size is 3″ in diameter. Stitch 2.
Square: Stitched on Plastic Canvas 14 over 1 mesh, the finished design size is 1¼″ x 1¼″. The canvas was cut 2″ x 2″ for each. Stitch 2.
Band: Stitched on Plastic Canvas 7 over 1 mesh, the finished design size is ¾″ x 9⅛″. The canvas was cut 2″ x 11″. Stitch 1.

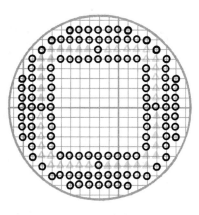

Circle for Ornament A
Stitch count: 20 x 20

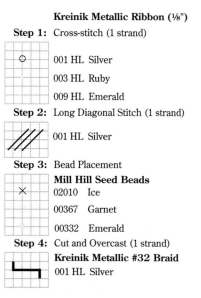

Kreinik Metallic Ribbon (⅛")

Step 1: Cross-stitch (1 strand)

⊙	001 HL Silver
	003 HL Ruby
	009 HL Emerald

Step 2: Long Diagonal Stitch (1 strand)

///	001 HL Silver

Step 3: Bead Placement

Mill Hill Seed Beads

✕	02010 Ice
	00367 Garnet
	00332 Emerald

Step 4: Cut and Overcast (1 strand)

Kreinik Metallic #32 Braid
001 HL Silver

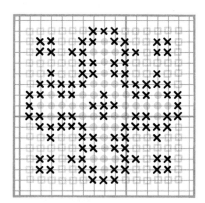

Square for Ornament A
Stitch count: 17 x 17

Band for Ornament A
Stitch count: 64 x 5

Sample for Ornament B

Stitched on Plastic Canvas 7 (4¼″ x 3⅛″) diamond over 1 mesh, the finished design size for 1 section is 1¼″ x 1¼″. Stitch 3 sections with ruby cross-stitches and 3 sections with emerald cross-stitches.

Ornament B
Stitch count: 9 x 9

Kreinik Metallic Ribbon (⅛″)

Step 1: Cross-stitch (1 strand)

003 HL Ruby
(stitch on 3 sections)

009 HL Emerald
(stitch on 3 sections)

Step 2: Scotch Stitch (1 strand)

001 HL Silver

Step 3: Bead Placement

Mill Hill Pebble Beads
■ 05021 Silver

Step 4: Cut and Overcast (1 strand)

Kreinik Metallic #32 Braid
001 HL Silver

Cap for Ornaments C and D
Stitch count: 11 x 11

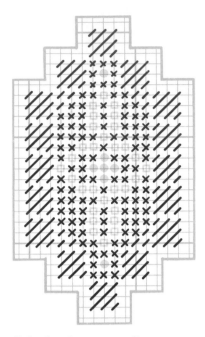

Side for Ornament C
Stitch count: 17 x 29

Sample for Ornament C

Stitched on Plastic Canvas 14 over 1 mesh, the finished design size is 1¼″ x 2⅛″ for 1 side and ¾″ x ¾″ for 1 cap. The canvas was cut 2½″ x 3¼″ for 1 side and 1½″ x 1½″ for 1 cap. Stitch 4 sides and 2 caps.

Kreinik Metallic #16 Braid

Step 1: Scotch Stitch (1 strand)

001 HL Silver

Step 2: Bead Placement

Mill Hill Seed Beads
× 02010 Ice
00367 Garnet
00332 Emerald

Step 3: Cut and Overcast (1 strand)

Kreinik Metallic #16 Braid
001 HL Silver

Sample for Ornament D

Stitched on Plastic Canvas 7 over 1 mesh, the finished design size is 2⅜″ x 4⅛″ for 1 side and 1⅝″ x 1⅝″ for 1 cap. The canvas was cut 4″ x 6″ for 1 side and 2½″ x 2½″ for 1 cap. Stitch

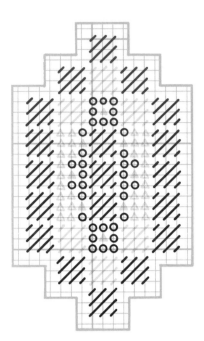

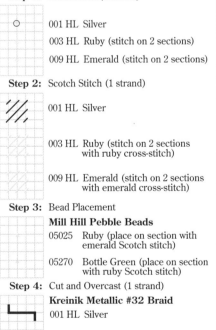

Side for Ornament D
Stitch count: 17 x 29

2 sides with ruby Scotch stitches and green beads, 2 sides with emerald Scotch stitches and ruby beads, and 2 caps.

Kreinik Metallic Ribbon (⅛″)

Step 1: Cross-stitch (1 strand)

○ 001 HL Silver

003 HL Ruby (stitch on 2 sections)

009 HL Emerald (stitch on 2 sections)

Step 2: Scotch Stitch (1 strand)

001 HL Silver

003 HL Ruby (stitch on 2 sections with ruby cross-stitch)

009 HL Emerald (stitch on 2 sections with emerald cross-stitch)

Step 3: Bead Placement

Mill Hill Pebble Beads

05025 Ruby (place on section with emerald Scotch stitch)

05270 Bottle Green (place on section with ruby Scotch stitch)

Step 4: Cut and Overcast (1 strand)

Kreinik Metallic #32 Braid
001 HL Silver

RIBBON EMBROIDERY ORNAMENTS

MATERIALS FOR EACH:
- Patterns on page 149
- 2 (6½″) squares of lightweight cardboard
- Embroidery needle
- Craft glue

For medallion:
- 6½″ x 7½″ piece of burgundy satin
- 6½″ x 7½″ piece of burgundy velvet
- 2 (9″) lengths of ¾″-wide burgundy satin ribbon
- 2 (9″) lengths of ½″-wide dusty rose satin ribbon
- 9″ (½″-wide) pink satin ribbon
- Thread: burgundy, dark pink, light pink
- DMC Size 5 pearl cotton thread: pink, dark green, lavender, lilac, yellow
- 1½ yards (⅛″-wide) pink satin ribbon
- ½ yard (¹⁄₁₆″-wide) burgundy satin ribbon
- 1¼ yards (⅛″-wide) olive satin ribbon
- 1 yard (⅛″-wide) light pink satin ribbon
- 1¼ yards (¹⁄₁₆″-wide) dusty rose satin ribbon
- ⅔ yard (⅛″) gold cording

For tree:
- 7″ x 8″ piece of purple satin
- 7″ x 8″ piece of purple velvet
- 2 (9″) lengths of ¾″-wide lavender satin ribbon
- 9″ (¾″-wide) lilac satin ribbon
- 3 (9″) lengths of ½″-wide purple satin ribbon
- 3 (9″) lengths of ½″-wide light pink satin ribbon
- 2 (9″) lengths of ½″-wide blue satin ribbon
- 3 (9″) lengths of ½″-wide bright pink satin ribbon
- Thread: purple, lavender, lilac, pink, blue

- DMC Size 5 pearl cotton thread: bright pink, light pink, tan, blue, light green, lavender, pink, purple, turquoise, yellow
- 2 yards (¹⁄₁₆″-wide) light green satin ribbon
- 2 yards (¹⁄₁₆″-wide) lilac satin ribbon
- 1¼ yards (¹⁄₁₆″-wide) light pink satin ribbon
- 20″ (⅜″) lavender satin corded piping
- 7″ (⅛″-wide) lavender satin braid

For wreath:
- 6½″ square of dark green satin
- 6½″ square of dark green velvet
- 3 (9″) lengths of ¾″-wide burgundy satin ribbon
- 3 (9″) lengths of ⅜″-wide pink satin ribbon

- 3 (9″) lengths of ⅜″-wide light pink satin ribbon
- 3 (9″) lengths of ⅜″-wide burgundy satin ribbon
- Thread: dark green, burgundy, pink, light pink
- DMC Size 5 pearl cotton thread: pink, dark pink, light pink, lavender, lilac, olive green, yellow
- 1 yard (⅛″-wide) dark green silk ribbon
- 1 yard (⅛″-wide) burgundy silk ribbon
- 1 yard (⅛″-wide) pink satin ribbon
- 1 yard (¹⁄₁₆″-wide) green satin ribbon
- 1 yard (¹⁄₁₆″-wide) pink satin ribbon
- 20″ (¼″-wide) green decorative braid
- 7″ (⅛″) matching green cording

DIRECTIONS

1. Prepare materials. For each: Transfer pattern and cut out as indicated. For ornament back, transfer pattern to satin and cut out, adding ½″ to outside edges. For ornament front, trace pattern in center of velvet, adding ½″ to all edges. Do not cut out.

2. Embellish ornament. (*Note:* 9″ ribbons are for ribbon flowers. Other ribbon amounts listed are to be used for raised rosestitches, lazy daisy stitches, and French knots.) **For each:** To make 1 ribbon flower, hold 1 end of a 9″ length of ribbon securely and twist ribbon with right side out (see Diagram A1). Beginning at 1 end, wrap ribbon to make a flower and pin to hold (see Diagram A2). Trim any excess ribbon. Make ribbon flowers in desired colors and ribbon widths and tack to velvet front with thread as shown in photo or as desired. Remove pins. Referring to Diagrams B, C, and D, fill in between ribbon flowers with ribbon and pearl

cotton raised rosestitches, lazy daisy stitches, and French knots as desired. Make lazy daisy stitches with ribbon and pearl cotton around outer edges of design as desired.

3. Complete ornament. For each: Cut out traced velvet shape. **For medallion:** Center 1 cardboard piece on wrong side of velvet and glue edges of velvet to back of cardboard. Beginning and ending at center top, glue gold cording around edges of velvet piece. Make a loop with 7″ length of remaining cording and glue to center top of cardboard for hanger. Center remaining cardboard piece on wrong side of satin and glue edges of satin to back of cardboard. With cardboard sides facing, glue velvet piece to satin piece. **For tree:** Using instructions for medallion, glue corded piping to wrong side around velvet piece. Fold braid in half to make a loop and glue to center top of cardboard for hanger. Finish ornament as for medallion.

For wreath: With matching thread, run a gathering thread around outside edge of velvet. Center 1 cardboard piece on wrong side of velvet. Pull to gather thread and secure; glue edges of velvet to back of cardboard. Clip and glue inside edge of velvet to back of cardboard. Glue braid around outer edge of velvet piece, overlapping ends. Repeat for inner edge. Fold cording in half to make a loop and glue ends to top back of cardboard for hanger. Finish ornament as for medallion.

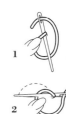

Ribbon Flower–Diagram A

Base Backstitch

Stemstitch

Side

Raised Rosestitch–Diagram B

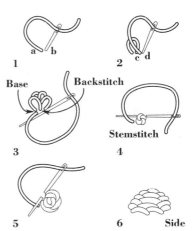

Lazy Daisy Stitch Diagram C

French Knot Diagram D

SNOWFLAKES

SNOWFLAKE WITH PEARLS

MATERIALS
- Completed cross-stitch designs on Plastic Canvas 10
- Thread: white, gold metallic
- 2 large pearl beads
- 9 medium pearl beads
- 42 small pearl beads
- 3 teardrop pearls
- Beading needle

DIRECTIONS
1. Make ornament top. With white thread, center and slipstitch 1 half piece A to each side of whole piece A to form a 4-sided ornament.

Sample for Snowflake with Pearls
Stitched on Plastic Canvas 10 over 1 mesh, the finished design size is 3¼″ x 3¾″. The canvas was cut 10″ x 10″. Cut and stitch 1 whole piece A, 2 half pieces A, 1 piece B, and 1 piece C. Complete Steps 1 and 2 of color code before beginning Directions.

Step 1: Cut and Overcast (1 strand)
Gold Dust
GD 10C   White Pearl (1 card)

Step 2: Long Stitch (1 strand)
Patina
PA 01   Natural (1 card)

Kreinik Metallics #8 Braid
002J   Japan Gold

Step 3: Bead Placement
Pearls
(see Steps 1 and 3 of Directions)

2. String and attach beads.
Referring to graph and using beading needle, secure white thread at top dot. String 1 large bead, 1 medium bead, and 4 small beads. Referring to graph and Diagram, thread needle through 1 side of ornament at 1 side dot, string 4 small beads and 1 medium bead, and reinsert needle through large bead and through top dot, making a loop. Pass needle again through large bead, and repeat to string medium and small beads in same manner for remaining 3 sides. Secure thread at top dot but do not cut.

3. Complete ornament. Bend and insert piece B through cutout center of piece C to form a 4-sided small ornament. Pick up beading needle, pass it again through large bead, string 4 small beads, remaining medium bead, and remaining large bead. Stitch to top of small ornament at dots. Secure and cut thread. String 3 small beads, 3 teardrop beads, and remaining 3 small beads. Stitch to bottom of small ornament at dots. Secure and cut thread. For hanger, sew a 6″ piece of gold metallic thread through top of large ornament and knot ends together to make a loop.

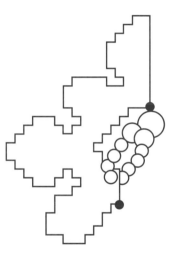

Diagram
One side of ornament only

Cut 1 piece A in half here.

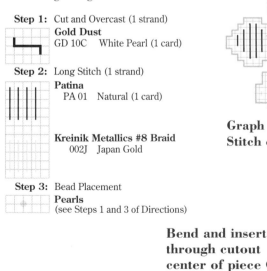

Graph for piece A
Stitch count: 34 x 27

Bend and insert through cutout center of piece C.

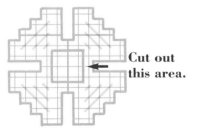

Cut out this area.

Graph for piece B
Stitch count: 11 x 11

Graph for piece C
Stitch count: 11 x 11

ESTAZ SNOWFLAKE

MATERIALS
- Completed cross-stitch designs on Plastic Canvas 10
- 172 (#02010) crystal Mill Hill seed beads
- 18 (#05161) crystal Mill Hill pebble beads
- Thread: white, gold metallic
- Beading needle

DIRECTIONS

1. Prepare materials. With beading needle and referring to graph, secure white thread at 1 dot on 1 point of whole piece. String 5 seed beads, 1 pebble bead, and 5 seed beads; secure thread at dot on opposite side of point across cutout area and cut thread. Repeat for remaining 7 points on whole piece and 3 whole points on each half piece.

2. Make ornament. With white thread, center and slipstitch 1 half piece to each side of whole piece to form a 4-sided ornament.

3. Complete ornament. With white thread and beading needle and referring to graph, secure thread at X. String 8 seed beads, 1 pebble bead, and 8 seed beads. Secure thread to opposite X across center of ornament. Repeat 3 times. For hanger, sew a 6″ piece of gold metallic thread through top of ornament and knot ends together to make a loop.

Sample for Estaz Snowflake
Stitched on Plastic Canvas 10 over 1 mesh, the finished design size is 4″. The plastic canvas was cut 10″ x 10″. Cut and stitch 1 whole piece and 2 half pieces. Complete Steps 1 and 2 of color code before beginning Directions.

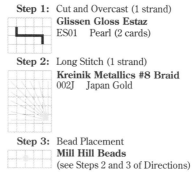

Step 1: Cut and Overcast (1 strand)
Glissen Gloss Estaz
ES01   Pearl (2 cards)

Step 2: Long Stitch (1 strand)
Kreinik Metallics #8 Braid
002J   Japan Gold

Step 3: Bead Placement
Mill Hill Beads
(see Steps 2 and 3 of Directions)

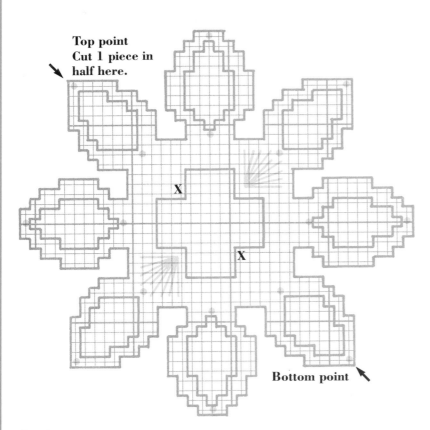

**Top point
Cut 1 piece in
half here.**

X

X

Bottom point

Stitch count: 40 x 39

CROSS-STITCHED SACHETS

MATERIALS (for 1)
- Completed cross-stitch design on cream Murano 30
- Thread to match fabric
- ½ yard (2¼″-wide) cream lace
- ¾ yard (¼″-wide) cream picot ribbon
- Polyester stuffing
- Small amount of potpourri

DIRECTIONS
1. Prepare materials. With design centered, trim Murano to 5¼″ x 6½″. With matching thread, machine-zigzag around all edges. Cut lace in half. Cut ribbon in half.

2. Make sachet. Run a gathering thread along straight edge of each lace piece. Pull to gather each lace piece to 5¼″ and secure. With right sides facing and edges aligned, stitch 1 piece of lace to each 5¼″ edge of fabric. With right sides facing and raw edges aligned, stitch long edges of fabric/lace piece together to make a tube. Turn. Knot 1 ribbon length around 1 end of tube over lace near seam and tie in a bow. Stuff ⅓ of sachet lightly, add potpourri to center, and finish stuffing. Tie remaining ribbon around end of sachet in same manner.

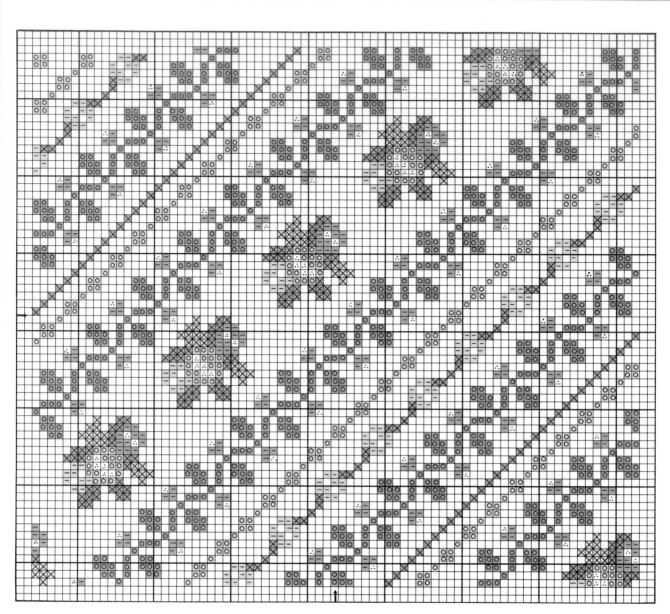

Stitch count: 70 x 79

Sample for Diagonal Design
Stitched on cream Murano 30 over 2 threads, the finished design size is 4⅝″ x 5¼″. The fabric was cut 8″ x 8″.

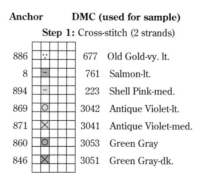

Anchor		DMC (used for sample)	
		Step 1: Cross-stitch (2 strands)	
886	∴	677	Old Gold-vy. lt.
8	−	761	Salmon-lt.
894	−	223	Shell Pink-med.
869	⊙	3042	Antique Violet-lt.
871	✕	3041	Antique Violet-med.
860	◎	3053	Green Gray
846	✕	3051	Green Gray-dk.

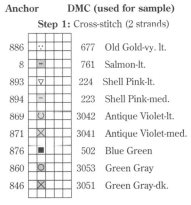

Stitch count: 55 x 78

Sample for Straight Design
Stitched on cream Murano 30 over 2
threads, the finished design size is 3⅝"
x 5¼". The fabric was cut 8" x 8".

Anchor		DMC (used for sample)	
		Step 1: Cross-stitch (2 strands)	
886	∴	677	Old Gold-vy. lt.
8	−	761	Salmon-lt.
893	▽	224	Shell Pink-lt.
894	−	223	Shell Pink-med.
869	○	3042	Antique Violet-lt.
871	✕	3041	Antique Violet-med.
876	■	502	Blue Green
860	○	3053	Green Gray
846	✕	3051	Green Gray-dk.

PLASTIC CANVAS JEWEL

MATERIALS
- Completed cross-stitch designs on Plastic Canvas 14
- 2 skeins of Marlitt #814 Plum-lt. embroidery floss
- 3″ x 7″ piece of cardboard
- Tapestry needle

DIRECTIONS

1. Assemble ornament. Cut out each cross-stitched piece 1 hole outside design. With 2 strands of plum floss, overcast-stitch 4 triangles together to form a pyramid. Repeat with remaining 4 triangles. Overcast-stitch pyramids together (see photo).

2. Complete ornament. For tassel, cut 1 (3″) and 1 (12″) piece of plum floss. Referring to Diagram A, tightly wind 1 skein of floss around cardboard. Thread needle with 3″ piece of floss. Referring to Diagram B, slide needle between cardboard and floss and tie 3″ piece of floss tightly around strands. Refer to Diagram C and cut untied ends of strands at opposite end of cardboard. Referring to Diagram D, form a narrow loop the desired length of finished wrap knot in 1 end of 12″ piece of floss; lay loop flat against tassel, with loop down and extending slightly below the area to be wrapped. Referring to Diagram E, evenly wrap strand around loop and bundle of strands, wrapping until loop is almost covered. Insert end of wrapping strand through bottom of loop (see Diagram E). Pull opposite end of strand to hide loop within knot. Use tapestry needle or a crochet hook to insert loose end of strand into tassel, hiding it (see Diagram F). Trim tassel to desired length and attach to 1 end of ornament with floss. For hanger, sew an 8″ piece of floss through top of ornament and knot ends together to make a loop.

Sample for Plastic Canvas Jewel

Stitched on Plastic Canvas 14 over 1 mesh, the finished design size is 2⅛" x 2⅛" for 1 motif. The canvas was cut 4" x 4". Stitch 8.

DMC		Marlitt (used for sample)
Step 1: Cross-stitch (2 strands)		
744		848 Yellow-pale
741		850 Tangerine-med.
3607		814 Plum-lt.
321		893 Christmas Red
552		858 Violet-dk.
826		835 Blue-med.
702		811 Kelly Green

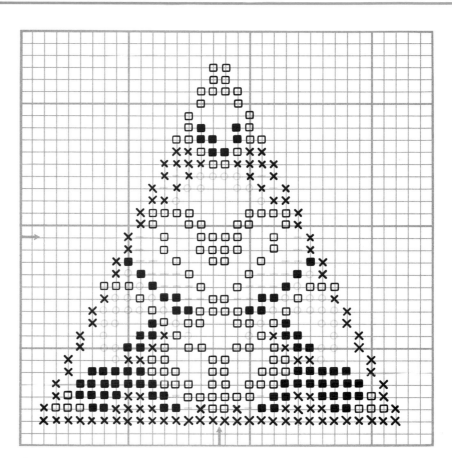

Stitch count: 30 x 30

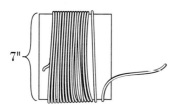

7"

Diagram A

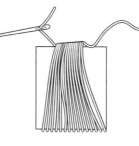

Diagram B

Diagram C

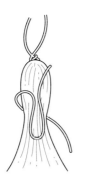

Diagram D

Diagram E

Diagram F

R IBBON FRAME

MATERIALS
- Mat board
- Craft knife
- Posterboard
- ¼ yard of pink satin moiré
- Scrap of fleece
- Craft glue
- 2 yards (⅜"-wide) light green silk ribbon
- 12" (⅜"-wide) flat ivory lace
- 1½ yards (⅝"-wide) pink picot satin ribbon
- 1½ yards (¾"-wide) pink satin ribbon
- Pink thread
- 19 (5-mm) pearl beads
- 2 yards (⅜"-wide) pink silk ribbon
- Monofilament

DIRECTIONS
1. Prepare materials. From mat board, cut 2 (5"-diameter) circles; from center of 1, cut 1 (2½"-diameter) circle. From posterboard, cut 2 (4½"-diameter) circles; from center of 1, cut 1 (3¼"-diameter) circle. From pink satin moiré, cut 2 (6"-diameter) circles; from center of 1, cut 1 (2¼"-diameter) circle. From fleece, cut 1 (5"-diameter) circle; from center, cut 1 (2½"-diameter) circle.

2. Make frame front. Glue fleece circle to mat board circle with cutout center. With right side up, center fabric circle with cutout center over fleece and glue fabric edges to back of board, clipping as necessary. Referring to Diagram A, loop and glue green ribbon around outer edge on wrong side of fabric/mat board circle. Glue 1 edge of lace trim around inner edge on wrong side of fabric/mat board circle so that lace extends beyond circle edge. Center and glue posterboard circle with cutout center to wrong side of fabric/mat board circle, covering raw edges. Set aside. Center and glue picot ribbon length to pink satin ribbon. Referring to

Diagram B, make ½"-wide box pleats along length of picot/satin ribbon. Stitch along center of ribbons to secure pleats. With picot ribbon up, glue center of pleated ribbon length to right side of fabric/mat board circle. Referring to photo and Diagram B, pinch and glue centers of each box pleat together. Center and glue 1 pearl between pleats. Set frame front aside.

3. Make frame back. With right side up, center remaining fabric circle over remaining mat board circle and glue fabric edges to back

of board, clipping as necessary. Referring to Diagram A, loop and glue pink silk ribbon around outer edge on wrong side of fabric/mat board circle. Center and glue remaining posterboard circle to wrong side of mat board circle.

4. Assemble frame. With wrong sides facing, glue bottom halves of frame front and frame back together. Insert desired photograph through top half of completed frame. For hanger, sew a 10" piece of monofilament through 1 ribbon loop at top of frame and knot ends together to make a loop.

Diagram A

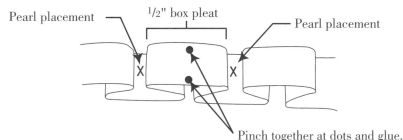

Pearl placement

½" box pleat

Pearl placement

Pinch together at dots and glue.

Diagram B

$\mathbf{P}$APER SNOWFLAKE AND ICICLE

SNOWFLAKE

MATERIALS (for 1)
- Completed cross-stitch designs on Perforated Paper 14
- Rubber cement
- Gold metallic thread

DIRECTIONS
Assemble snowflake. Cut out each design along lines indicated on graph. Overlap unstitched ends of hexagon tips and arrange in snowflake design (see photo). Glue ends together. Glue square motif to center of ornament. For hanger, sew a 6″ piece of gold metallic thread through 1 hexagon tip and knot ends together to make a loop.

Sample for Snowflake
Stitched on white Perforated Paper 14 over 1 thread, the finished design sizes are ½″ x ½″ for square motif and 1⅜″ x 1¼″ for hexagon tip. The paper was cut 4″ x 4″ for each. Stitch 1 square motif and 8 hexagon tips.

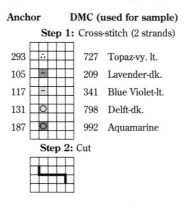

Anchor		DMC (used for sample)	
Step 1: Cross-stitch (2 strands)			
293		727	Topaz-vy. lt.
105		209	Lavender-dk.
117		341	Blue Violet-lt.
131		798	Delft-dk.
187		992	Aquamarine
Step 2: Cut			

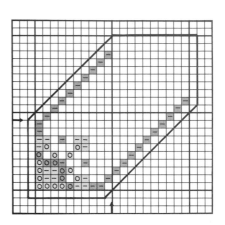

Stitch count: 20 x 18

Stitch count: 7 x 7

ICICLE

MATERIALS (for 1)
- Completed cross-stitch designs on Perforated Paper 14
- Rubber cement
- 1 (3″) purchased aquamarine cotton tassel
- 1 (⅜″) light green ball button
- Gold metallic thread

DIRECTIONS
Assemble icicle. Cut out each design along lines indicated on graph. Overlap motifs as shown in photo and glue. Tie tassel through hole in button. Glue button to bottom of ornament. For hanger, sew a 6″ piece of gold metallic thread through top of ornament and knot ends together to make a loop.

Sample for Icicle
Stitched on white Perforated Paper 14 over 1 thread, the finished design size is 1″ x 1¼″ for 1 motif. The paper was cut 4″ x 4″. Stitch 3 motifs.

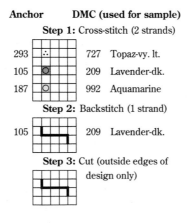

Anchor		DMC (used for sample)	
Step 1: Cross-stitch (2 strands)			
293		727	Topaz-vy. lt.
105		209	Lavender-dk.
187		992	Aquamarine
Step 2: Backstitch (1 strand)			
105		209	Lavender-dk.
Step 3: Cut (outside edges of design only)			

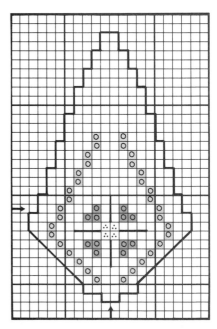

Stitch count: 14 x 17

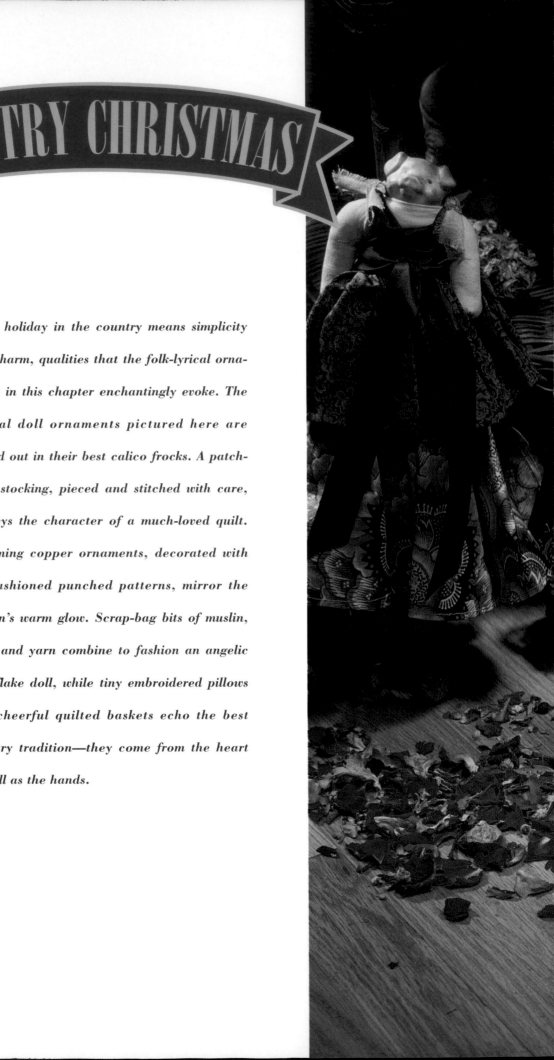

COUNTRY CHRISTMAS

The holiday in the country means simplicity and charm, qualities that the folk-lyrical ornaments in this chapter enchantingly evoke. The animal doll ornaments pictured here are turned out in their best calico frocks. A patchwork stocking, pieced and stitched with care, conveys the character of a much-loved quilt. Gleaming copper ornaments, decorated with old-fashioned punched patterns, mirror the season's warm glow. Scrap-bag bits of muslin, lace, and yarn combine to fashion an angelic snowflake doll, while tiny embroidered pillows and cheerful quilted baskets echo the best country tradition—they come from the heart as well as the hands.

ANIMAL DOLL

MATERIALS (for 1)
- Patterns on page 152
- Greenware bear, pig, or rabbit head*
- Acrylic paints in colors of choice
- Small and medium paintbrushes
- Acrylic spray matte finish
- 6" x 8" piece of print fabric for body
- 2 (3¾" x 11") pieces of print fabric for legs
- Thread to match fabrics
- Stuffing
- Assorted fabric prints for clothing
- Eyelet fabric (optional)
- Black fabric for mittens (optional)
- Assorted novelty yarns and ribbons

DIRECTIONS

Patterns include ¼" seam allowance except where otherwise indicated. *Note:* Instructions below are general and models in photo are examples only; improvise doll's clothing and accessories as desired.

1. Prepare ceramic head. Have greenware head fired at a ceramic shop. Paint head with desired base color. Let dry. Referring to photo, paint details on head as desired. Let dry. Spray head with acrylic matte finish.

2. Make doll body. Transfer pattern for body and cut out as indicated. With right sides facing, stitch darts and press. With right sides facing and raw edges aligned, stitch body pieces together, leaving open as indicated on pattern. Turn. Fold under ¼" around neck. Insert head into neck opening. Stitch to reinforce shoulder seams and secure head. With right sides facing and raw edges aligned, fold 1 leg piece in half lengthwise. Stitch, rounding 1 end like arm and leaving other end open. Turn and press. With seam at side, on front of leg, center and stitch a ¼" tuck parallel to seam. Stuff leg firmly to within ½" of open end and baste opening closed. Repeat for other leg. Turn under ¼" around bottom of body. With tucks at front, place leg tops inside opening and stitch to body front only. Stuff body firmly. Slipstitch opening closed, catching legs in seam.

3. Make doll clothing. Use print body as blouse or wrap upper body in 1"-wide ribbon and tie fabric strips at shoulders. If desired, crisscross folded ¾" x 5" strips over shoulders and tack to body. For sleeves, cut 2 (2" x 6") print strips; stitch ends and slip over arms. Slipstitch to body and make a tuck in top near outer edge of each sleeve. If desired, transfer pattern for mittens and cut out as indicated. With right sides facing and raw edges aligned, stitch mitten pieces together, leaving straight edges open. Turn and stuff. Turn under raw edges and stitch 1 mitten to each arm. For collar ruff, cut a 3" x 15" strip. Fold in half lengthwise, with wrong sides together. Run a gathering thread along long raw edges and gather to fit neck. Secure and tack at neck. For shawl or apron, cut a 9" x 12" right triangle from print and tie around waist or over shoulders as desired. For skirt, cut an 11" x 31" strip for full-length or an 8" x 31" for calf-length and, if desired, a 7" x 31" strip for eyelet overskirt or 5" x 31" strip of print for short overskirt. Hem each skirt bottom; run 2 gathering threads along skirt top. Place skirt on doll, gather to fit waist, and stitch skirt to body at waistline. Fringe short print overskirt by making 1½" clips every ¼" and knotting strips together in pairs. Wind novelty yarn several times around ankles and knot.

Rabbit Doll wants to be your Easter Bunny! Place her in a shallow basket on cellophane grass and surround her with gaily colored eggs for an appealing centerpiece.

*Available from Chapelle Limited, P.O. Box 9252, Newgate Station, Ogden, UT 84409.

PUNCHED COPPER ORNAMENTS

MATERIALS FOR EACH:
- Patterns on page 153
- Tracing paper
- Masking tape
- 3½″ square of ¼″ plywood
- Copper scraps for practice
- 2¾″ square of medium-weight copper
- Center punch
- Lightweight hammer
- Screwdriver
- Tin snips
- Metal cleaner
- Fine-grade steel wool (optional)
- Acrylic spray finish (optional)
- 2 (4″) squares of fabric
- Thread to match fabric
- Small amount of stuffing
- ½ yard (1⁄16″-wide) contrasting satin ribbon

For heart:
- 4 (5-mm) pink heart beads
- 2 (5-mm) lavender heart beads
- Embroidery floss: lavender, cream

For square:
- 12 (4-mm) gold glass beads
- Aqua embroidery floss

DIRECTIONS
All seam allowances are ¼″. *Note:* Working on plywood square, practice punching with copper scraps to determine number and force of taps needed to produce a uniform design. Use center punch to punch holes, punching through tracing paper pattern and copper. Use hammer and screwdriver to score lines without punching through copper.

1. Make punched design. For each: Trace pattern to tracing paper. Center pattern on copper square and tape to secure. Place copper on plywood square and punch design in copper according to pattern. Add 1 hole ¼″ from each corner of square for tacking copper to pillow. Wash punched copper in soapy water. Use metal cleaner to remove any fingerprints. If a satin finish is desired, polish copper with fine-grade steel wool and then spray it with acrylic finish.

2. Make pillow. For each: With right sides facing, stitch fabric squares together, leaving a small opening. Clip, turn, and stuff firmly. Slipstitch opening closed.

3. Assemble ornament. For heart: Referring to photo, use 2 strands of cream floss to sew beads to punched design. Tie ends of floss in bow at top center of heart. Center copper on pillow and tack to pillow through corner holes, using 2 strands of lavender floss. **For square:** Referring to photo, use 2 strands of aqua floss to make long stitches between holes in large square and holes in small square, attaching beads around small square and attaching copper square to pillow as for heart.

4. Complete ornament. For each: Cut a 13″ length from ribbon and tie in a double bow. Center bow on 1 edge of pillow and tack in place. For hanger, fold remaining ribbon in half and knot ends together to make a loop. Tack knot to back of ornament.

Having a cozy Christmas gathering? For party mementoes, make the punched copper squares only. Tie a ribbon hanger through the top holes of each square, add a name and the year to each, and hand them out as your guests depart.

QUILTED BASKETS

MATERIALS (for 1)

- Patterns on page 152
- Scraps of dark red and light red prints
- ⅛ yard of solid red fabric
- Thread to match fabrics
- 5″ square of medium cardboard
- Craft glue
- White embroidery floss
- Scrap of batting
- 7 (6-mm) blue-green barrel pony beads
- ½ yard (⅜″-wide) grosgrain ribbon

DIRECTIONS

Patterns include ¼″ seam allowance.

1. Prepare materials. Transfer all patterns and cut out as indicated. From solid red fabric, cut ½″-wide bias strips, piecing as need to make a 52″ strip.

2. Make handle. To cover cardboard handle, wrap red bias strip around it, overlapping fabric edges ¼″, until handle is covered. Glue ends in place. Set aside.

3. Make basket. For front, referring to Piecing Diagram and photo, with right sides facing and raw edges aligned, join triangles. With right sides facing and raw edges aligned, join base to bottom edge of pieced basket. Using 1 strand of white embroidery floss and referring to Piecing Diagram, blanket-stitch designated triangles. Using front as a pattern, cut 1 from print scrap for back and 1 from batting. Stack batting, front (right side up), and back (right side down). Using ¼″ seam, stitch around edges of basket, leaving top edge open. Trim batting from seam. Clip corners. Turn. Turn under ¼″ along top edges of basket. Insert ends of handle ½″ into basket. Slipstitch opening closed, catching handle fabric in seam. Referring to Piecing

Diagram, tack basket through all layers at dots.

4. Complete ornament. Referring to photo, stitch beads to top of basket. For hanger, loop ribbon through handle and knot ends together to make a hanger loop.

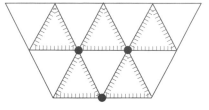

Piecing Diagram

![T]WIG WREATH

MATERIALS
- 14 bunches of approximately 12 (7"-long) thin twigs each
- 4 yards (18-gauge) florist's wire
- 4"-diameter metal ring
- 14" (⅝"-wide) variegated wired-edge ribbon
- Twig with dried berries
- Assorted small dried flowers
- Small amount of purchased dried moss
- Assorted porcelain flowers
- Decorative trims
- Low-temperature glue gun and glue stick

DIRECTIONS
1. Make wreath. Wrap 1 end of 1 bunch of twigs with florist's wire. Repeat for remaining bunches. Place wired end of 1 twig bunch on metal ring and wire to ring. Referring to photo, continue in same manner with remaining bunches, overlapping bunches to cover wired ends. Fill in gaps in wreath with additional twigs or bunches. Fan out twigs on outside of wreath.

2. Embellish wreath. Tie ribbon in a bow and wire to wreath with florist's wire. Glue a cluster of flowers in center of bow. Glue dried materials, porcelain flowers, and decorative trims to wreath as desired (see photo). For hanger, twist a 4" piece of florist's wire into a loop and attach to wire ring.

SANTA SACK

MATERIALS
- Completed cross-stitch design on Rustico 14
- ¼ yard of unstitched Rustico 14
- ¼ yard of burgundy lining fabric
- Thread to match fabrics
- 1 yard (⅜″-wide) cream picot ribbon

DIRECTIONS
All seams are ¼″.

1. Prepare materials. With design centered, trim design piece to 7½″ x 8½″. From unstitched Rustico, cut 1 (7½″ x 8½″) piece for back and 1 (3½″ x 26½″) piece for ruffle. From lining fabric, cut 2 (7½″ x 8½″) pieces and 1 (3½″ x 26½″) piece.

2. Make sack. With right sides facing and raw edges aligned, stitch design piece to back piece along side and bottom edges. To make a boxed bottom, at 1 bottom corner of bag, align side and bottom seams by flattening bag, with right sides facing and with 1 seam on top of the other; finger-press seam allowances open. Referring to Diagram, stitch across each corner. Clip corners and turn. Repeat for lining front and back, except leave a 4″ opening in 1 side. Do not turn. With right sides facing and seams aligned, stitch ends of Rustico ruffle piece together. Run a gathering thread along 1 long raw edge of ruffle and gather to fit top edge of Rustico bag. With right sides facing and raw edges aligned, stitch ruffle to bag. Repeat for lining ruffle and bag. With right sides facing and seams aligned, slide lining over bag. Stitch lining to bag around top edge of

ruffle. Turn through opening in side of lining. Slipstitch opening closed. Tuck lining inside bag. Fill bag as desired and tie ribbon around top.

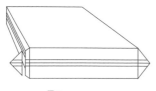

Diagram

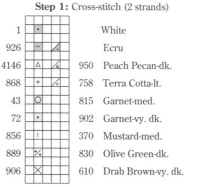

Anchor			DMC (used for sample)	
Step 1: Cross-stitch (2 strands)				
1	•			White
926	–	◿		Ecru
4146	△	◿	950	Peach Pecan-dk.
868	+	◿	758	Terra Cotta-lt.
43	○		815	Garnet-med.
72	•		902	Garnet-vy. dk.
856	ı		370	Mustard-med.
889	⫽		830	Olive Green-dk.
906	✕		610	Drab Brown-vy. dk.

Sample for Santa Sack
Stitched on Rustico 14 over 1 thread, the finished design size is 3⅝″ x 5¼″. The fabric was cut 10″ x 11″.

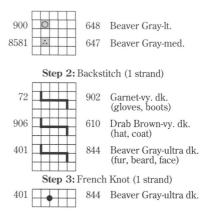

900	○		648	Beaver Gray-lt.
8581	⣿		647	Beaver Gray-med.

Step 2: Backstitch (1 strand)

72		902	Garnet-vy. dk. (gloves, boots)
906		610	Drab Brown-vy. dk. (hat, coat)
401		844	Beaver Gray-ultra dk. (fur, beard, face)

Step 3: French Knot (1 strand)

401	●	844	Beaver Gray-ultra dk.

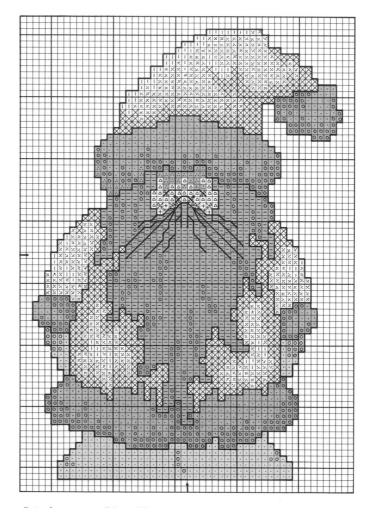

Stitch count: 50 x 73

QUILTED STOCKING

MATERIALS
- Patterns on page 153
- ⅛ yard of dark green print fabric
- Fabric scraps: heavy cotton, muslin, burgundy-and-white stripe in wide and narrow sizes, bright pink, light pink, cream/red print
- Scrap of fleece
- Dressmaker's pen
- Thread to match fabrics
- Embroidery floss: aqua, dark green, white
- 3 assorted white buttons
- 8 (3-mm) green pebble beads
- ¾ yard (1″-wide) pink bias tape

DIRECTIONS
Stocking pattern is full-size. Add ¼″ seam allowances to appliqué pieces as indicated.

1. Prepare materials. Transfer whole stocking pattern and markings and cut out as indicated. Transfer appliqué patterns and cut out as indicated. From dark green print, cut 1 (2¼″ x 5″) piece for front cuff. From light pink fabric, cut 2 (¾″ x 1¼″) pieces. From narrow burgundy-and-white stripe, cut 1 (1″ x 1¼″) piece.

2. Make stocking front. Referring to pattern and photo, appliqué fans, center piece, 2 narrow burgundy-and-white striped squares, toe, and heel to heavy cotton stocking (background) piece. Sew light pink pieces to sides of remaining narrow burgundy-and-white striped piece and trim new piece to 1 (1¼″) square. Referring to pattern and photo, set this square on the diagonal and appliqué to background stocking. Stack muslin stocking, fleece, and background stocking (right side up). With white thread, quilt as shown on pattern.

3. Embellish stocking front. Embroider stocking as follows: With 2 strands of aqua floss, satin-stitch band across upper top of stocking 1″ from top edge. With 2 strands of dark green floss, couch across aqua band at 1/16″ intervals. With 2 strands of white floss, satin-stitch 1 small circle to bottom point of each fan. With 2 strands of dark green floss, satin-stitch and then backstitch 1 arrow point to right of right fan and 1 arrow point to left of left fan. With 2 strands of dark green floss, outline-stitch along top of center piece. With 2 strands of dark green floss, outline-stitch zigzag patterns on bottom half of stocking as shown on pattern. Attach buttons and beads as indicated on pattern.

4. Complete stocking. With wrong sides facing and long edges matching, fold cuff piece in half lengthwise and press. Place fold over top edge of heavy cotton stocking. Fold under ¼″ on each long edge of cuff and slipstitch to stocking. With right sides facing and raw edges aligned, stitch 2 green print stocking pieces together along top edge only. Turn and press. Place stocking front (right side up) on green print stocking and baste raw edges together. Bind raw edges with bias tape and form a 1½″ hanger loop at upper right end of stocking. Tuck end under and slipstitch to tape in back.

Think of the nifty surprises this pretty stocking could hold: some crisp new bills, favorite candy, a beautiful bookmark, maybe a treasured snapshot. Whatever you choose, this present is sure to please—handmade is made with love.

PLEASANT PEASANTS

MATERIALS FOR EACH:
- Patterns on page 154
- 2"-diameter craft foam ball
- 4"-diameter craft foam ball
- Small paring knife
- Low-temperature glue gun and glue stick
- 1¼ yards of medium cotton cording
- Brown embroidery floss
- Embroidery needle
- Colored pencils: red, brown
- Small amount of stuffing
- 12" of brown rayon braid

For woman:
- Fabric scraps: blue, rose print, cream, muslin, rose, burgundy, brown paisley
- Thread to match fabrics
- Dark blue embroidery floss
- 2 different (⅜"-wide) buttons

For man:
- Fabric scraps: cream, muslin, maroon, light blue print, brown stripe
- Thread to match fabrics
- 3 (⅜") purple buttons
- 3" navy braid
- Auburn crepe hair
- ⅜ yard (⅛"-wide) maroon satin ribbon

DIRECTIONS
Patterns include ¼" seam allowance.

1. Prepare materials. For each: Transfer patterns and cut out as indicated. **For woman:** Cut 1 (2" x 4") rectangle from rose fabric for shirt. Cut 1 (2½" x 7") rectangle from burgundy fabric for jacket. Cut 1 (3½" x 7½") rectangle from brown paisley for hat. **For man:** Cut 1 (2¼" x 9½") rectangle from maroon fabric for shirt. Cut 1 (2½"-diameter) circle from blue print for hat. Cut 1 (2½" x 3½") rectangle from blue print for undervest. Cut 1 (3" x 8½") rectangle from brown stripe fabric for jacket.

2. Make body. For each: Using paring knife, cut and discard a slice about the size of a quarter from 2" craft foam ball. Cut and discard a slice about the size of a half-dollar from 4" ball. Glue cut sides of balls together to make body and head. Starting at bottom of body, coil and glue cording continuously around balls to top of head. **For woman:** Using 2 strands of blue floss, cross-stitch eyes on face piece. **For man:** Using 2 strands of brown floss, cross-stitch eyes on face piece. **For each:** Referring to photo, draw cheeks, mouth, and nose on face with colored pencils. Turn under seam allowance and center face on head ½" above body. Slipstitch face to head.

3. Make and attach clothing. For woman: Turn under seam allowance on shawl, vest, and jacket; press. Center shirt at top of body below face and slipstitch top and bottom edges to cording. Center jacket on back of body, overlapping shirt in front, and slipstitch in place. Center vest on shirt and slipstitch edges, easing top edge to fit. Tack 1 button on center of vest. **For man:** Center undervest on body below face with 3½" edge at neck. Turn under seam allowance on bottom of undervest and slipstitch undervest to body. Make a ½" tuck in center front at neck and tack. Center shirt on back of body, overlapping undervest in front and placing bottom edge ¼" below undervest. Turn under seam allowances on ends and bottom and slipstitch to body. Turn under seam allowance on jacket. Run a gathering thread along 1 long edge. Position jacket on body with gathering stitch at neck. Gather to fit neck and secure thread. Slipstitch other edges to body. Glue buttons down 1 side of shirt.

4. Make and attach sleeves and hands. For each: With right sides facing, stitch 2 sleeve pieces together, leaving long straight end open. Turn and stuff lightly. Turn under seam allow-ance and slipstitch opening closed. With right sides facing, stitch 2 hand pieces together, leaving straight edge open; turn and press. Referring to photo, position hand on body. Stitch straight edge only to body. Slipstitch sleeve in place. Repeat for remaining hand and sleeve.

5. Make and attach hat. For woman: With right sides facing, stitch ends of paisley rectangle together. Turn. Turn under seam allowances on long edges. Run a gathering thread along 1 edge. Pull to gather tightly and secure. Sew remaining button to gathered edge. Place hat on head and slipstitch in place. Referring to photo, tack gather-ed edge of hat to 1 side of head. **For man:** Run a gathering thread ⅛" from outside edge of hat and pull to gather. Flatten hat. (It should be about 2" in diameter.) Secure thread. Fold navy braid in half and tack fold to top of hat. Fray braid ends and trim. Separate crepe hair and glue to head. Glue hat to top of head.

6. Complete ornament. For woman: Referring to photo and using 2 strands of brown floss, stitch small loops around face for hair. Fringe short edges of shawl ⅛". Place shawl on doll and knot ends together at neck front. **For man:** Wrap ribbon around neck, knot in front as for a man's tie, and tack ends. **For each:** For hanger, sew brown braid through top of ornament and knot ends togeth-er to make a loop.

CHRISTMAS BEARS

MATERIALS (for 1)
- Patterns on page 155
- ¼ yard of plaid fabric
- Scrap of black fabric
- Thread to match plaid
- 5 pairs (30-mm) doll joints
- Stuffing
- 1" x 12" strip of wool or 1½ yards of yarn for scarf

DIRECTIONS
Patterns include ¼" seam allowance.

1. Prepare materials. Transfer patterns and markings and cut out as indicated.

2. Make head. With right sides facing and raw edges aligned, stitch 2 ear pieces together, leaving bottom edge open as indicated on pattern. Turn. Make a small tuck at bottom center of ear. Repeat with remaining ear pieces.

With right sides facing and raw edges aligned, match A and B on top head piece to A and B on 1 side head piece and stitch together. Repeat with other side head piece, except leave a 1" opening at back of head. With right sides facing, stitch head pieces together from A down front of neck, across bottom of neck, and up to B. Referring to pattern, make 1 small slit on each side of head for ears. Matching raw edges, insert 1 ear into 1 slit. With right sides facing, stitch a narrow seam to secure ear. Repeat with other ear. Turn through opening in back of head. Following manufacturer's instructions, insert shank of doll joint through bottom of neck at X. Stuff head firmly and slipstitch opening closed.

3. Complete body. With right sides facing, match dots and stitch 1 paw piece to 1 inside arm piece. With right sides facing, stitch inside arm piece to 1 outside arm piece, leaving an opening. Turn. Referring to pattern for placement, insert shank of doll joint at X. Stuff firmly and slipstitch opening closed. Repeat for other arm.

With right sides facing, stitch 2 leg pieces together, leaving an opening on 1 side seam and at bottom edge of leg as indicated. With right sides facing, stitch 1 sole piece to bottom of leg. Turn and, referring to pattern for placement, insert shank of doll joint at X. Stuff firmly and slipstitch opening closed. Repeat for other leg.

With right sides facing, stitch body pieces together, leaving an opening in back as indicated. Turn. Place lock washers only inside body at Xs and attach legs, head, and arms, referring to patterns for placement. Stuff body firmly and slipstitch opening closed.

4. Complete ornament. To make scarf from wool, pull threads from each end to make ½" fringe. Tie scarf around bear's neck. To make scarf from yarn, cut yarn into 3 (18") lengths and knot 1 end of all 3 lengths together. Braid yarn, knot ends, and tie scarf around neck.

Give Christmas Bears a place of honor at your family holiday table! Cradle a place card in each seated bear's arms and then let the bears go home with their dinner partners as souvenirs.

HOLIDAY BOW

MATERIALS
- ¼ yard of cranberry fabric
- 4½" x 6" piece of light green fabric
- Thread to match fabrics
- 1¾" x 4¼" piece of lightweight cardboard
- 1¼ yards (⅛"-wide) light green satin ribbon
- 5 (3-mm) green glass beads

DIRECTIONS
All seams are ¼".

1. Prepare materials. Cut 1 (5" x 15") and 2 (¾" x 6") strips from cranberry fabric. Cut 1 (1½" x 2½"), 1 (1½" x 4½"), and 2 (¾" x 6") strips from green fabric.

2. Make bow. With right sides facing and raw edges aligned, fold 5" x 15" cranberry strip in half widthwise. Stitch long side edges together, leaving bottom end open. Turn. Insert and center cardboard, with 4¼" edge of cardboard parallel to 5" edge of fabric. Turn under seam allowance and slipstitch opening closed. Referring to Diagram A, run gathering threads close to both side edges, down center front, and then center back. Pull center threads to gather fabric tightly around cardboard and secure. Pull side threads slightly to shape bow and secure.

3. Make checkerboard center. With right sides facing and raw edges aligned, sew ¾" x 6" strips together along long edges as shown in Diagram B to form a pieced band. Trim seams to ⅛". Cutting across seams, cut band into 8 (¾"-wide) strips. With right sides facing and raw edges aligned, sew strips together, alternating colors, to make a checkerboard band (see Diagram C).

4. Complete ornament. With right sides facing and raw edges aligned, stitch 1 end of checkerboard band to 1 end of 1½" x 2½" green strip to make a 4½"-long strip. With right sides facing, stitch checkerboard/green strip to 1½" x 4½" green strip along both long edges. Turn. Fold 1 end of checkerboard band under ¼". Center and wrap checkerboard band, with checkerboard up, around center of bow. Tuck raw end of checkerboard band snugly inside folded end and slipstitch. Cut 2 (13") lengths of ribbon. Wrap 1 piece around bow to left of checkerboard band and tie in a bow in front. Repeat on right side of checkerboard band. Referring to photo, stitch beads in a cluster to checkerboard band. For hanger, fold remaining length of ribbon in half. Knot ends together and make a knot 3" from top of ribbon loop. Tack ends to center back of ornament.

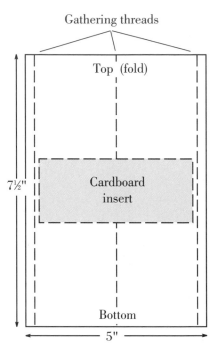

Diagram A

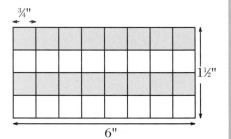

Diagram B

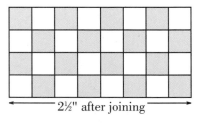

Diagram C

NEEDLEPOINT FRUIT

MATERIALS (for 3)
- Completed needlepoint designs on Needlepoint Canvas 14
- Thread to match
- Stuffing
- 3 yards (¼") green-and-gold braided cording
- Hot-glue gun and glue stick

DIRECTIONS
Patterns include ¼" seam allowance.

1. Make ornament. Cut out design pieces, adding ¼" seam allowance. With right sides facing and edges aligned, stitch design front to back, leaving an opening for turning. Turn and stuff firmly. Slipstitch opening closed. Referring to

photo for placement, tack 1 leaf to top of apple and 2 leaves each to top of pear and peach.

2. Complete ornament. Cut cording into 3 (1-yard) pieces. For 1 hanger, cut a 3" length from 1 (1-yard) piece and fold remaining length in half. With matching thread, tack braid together 4" from cut ends. To make tassel, glue 1 end of 3" length over tacking; wrap length tightly around doubled braid several times and glue to secure. Unravel cut ends of braid. Referring to photo, tack braid to back of ornament. Repeat to make hangers for remaining ornaments.

LEAF

Stitched on Needlepoint Canvas 14 over 1 thread, the finished design size is ¾" x 1⅜". The canvas was cut 5" x 5". Stitch 10 leaves.

DMC		Marlitt (used for sample)	
Step 1: Continental Stitch (6 strands)			
703	–	810	Chartreuse
702	✕	811	Kelly Green
890	○	853	Pistachio Green-ultra dk.

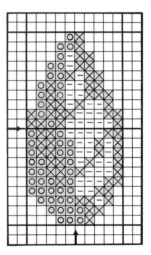

Stitch count: 10 x 20

PEAR

Stitched on Needlepoint Canvas 14 over 1 thread, the finished design size is 2⅜" x 3⅜". The canvas was cut 6" x 6". Stitch 2 pears.

DMC		Marlitt (used for sample)	
Step 1: Continental Stitch (6 strands)			
744	∴	848	Yellow-pale
726	□	867	Topaz-lt.
741	▫	849	Tangerine-med.
740	⠂	850	Tangerine
472	✕	1029	Avocado Green-ultra lt.
734	✕	1011	Olive Green-lt.

Stitch count: 34 x 47

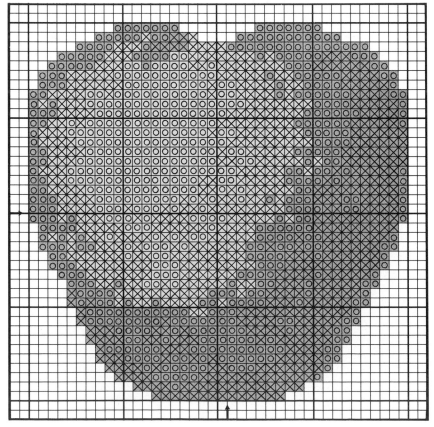

Stitch count: 42 x 40

Stitch count: 40 x 40

PEACH

Stitched on Needlepoint Canvas 14 over 1 thread, the finished design size is 3″ x 2⅞″. The canvas was cut 6″ x 6″. Stitch 2 peaches.

DMC		Marlitt (used for sample)	
		Step 1: Continental Stitch (6 strands)	
754	−	1042	Peach-lt.
3708	○	830	Melon-lt.
3706	−	831	Melon-med.
223	○	1207	Shell Pink-med.

APPLE

Stitched on Needlepoint Canvas 14 over 1 thread, the finished design size is 2⅞″ x 2⅞″. The canvas was cut 6″ x 6″. Stitch 2 apples.

DMC		Marlitt (used for sample)	
		Step 1: Continental Stitch (6 strands)	
947	○	1057	Burnt Orange
606	✕	1017	Orange Red-bright
321	○	843	Christmas Red
816	✕	894	Garnet

CROSS-STITCHED CIRCLES

MATERIALS (for 1)
- Completed cross-stitch design on clay Linda 27
- Thread to match
- 4"-diameter circle of polyester fleece
- 3½"-diameter wooden ring
- Craft glue
- 3"-diameter circle of matching fabric
- 1 (½") contrasting button
- ¾ yard (1/16"-wide) gray rayon braid
- 5 (7-mm) plastic beads
- 2 (3-mm) white jingle bells

DIRECTIONS

1. Prepare materials. With design centered, trim design piece to a 6½"-diameter circle. Machine-zigzag edges of design piece and then sew running stitch around edges (do not cut thread).

2. Make ornament. Center and glue fleece to 1 side of wooden ring. Center design piece, right side up, on fleece. Gather thread tightly around ring and secure. Turn edges of matching fabric circle under ¼" and slip-stitch to center back of ornament.

3. Embellish ornament. Sew button to center of design through all layers. Cut 1 (22") length from braid; fold in half and tack fold to center top of ornament. Thread 3 beads onto remaining 5" braid length and tie a knot 1" from ends. Thread 1 jingle bell onto each end and knot ends. Thread 1 end of 22" braid length through loop with beads and bells; knot braid ½" from top of ornament, add remaining 2 beads, and knot again above beads. Knot ends together to make a loop.

119

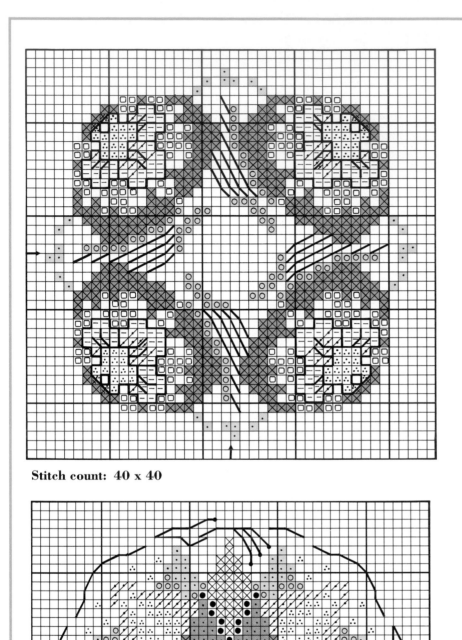

Stitch count: 40 x 40

BEIGE CIRCLE

Stitched on clay Linda 27 over 2 threads, the finished design size is 3″ x 3″. The fabric was cut 8″ x 8″.

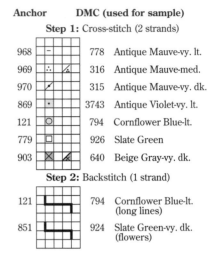

Anchor		DMC (used for sample)	
		Step 1: Cross-stitch (2 strands)	
968	−	778	Antique Mauve-vy. lt.
969	∴ ⁄	316	Antique Mauve-med.
970	⁄	315	Antique Mauve-vy. dk.
869	·	3743	Antique Violet-vy. lt.
121	○	794	Cornflower Blue-lt.
779	▢	926	Slate Green
903	⊠ ⁄	640	Beige Gray-vy. dk.
		Step 2: Backstitch (1 strand)	
121		794	Cornflower Blue-lt. (long lines)
851		924	Slate Green-vy. dk. (flowers)

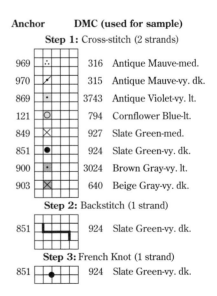

Stitch count: 41 x 41

BLUE CIRCLE

Stitched on clay Linda 27 over 2 threads, the finished design size is 3″ x 3″. The fabric was cut 8″ x 8″.

Anchor		DMC (used for sample)	
		Step 1: Cross-stitch (2 strands)	
969	∴	316	Antique Mauve-med.
970	⁄	315	Antique Mauve-vy. dk.
869	·	3743	Antique Violet-vy. lt.
121	○	794	Cornflower Blue-lt.
849	⊠	927	Slate Green-med.
851	●	924	Slate Green-vy. dk.
900	·	3024	Brown Gray-vy. lt.
903	⊠	640	Beige Gray-vy. dk.
		Step 2: Backstitch (1 strand)	
851		924	Slate Green-vy. dk.
		Step 3: French Knot (1 strand)	
851	●	924	Slate Green-vy. dk.

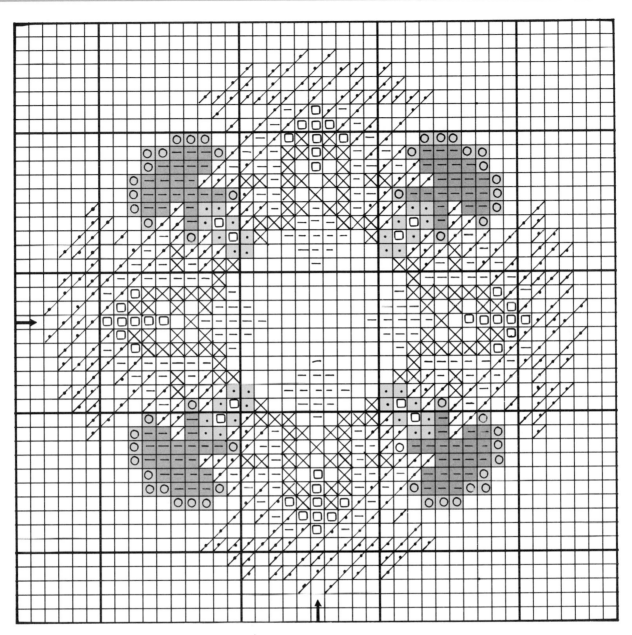

Stitch count: 39 x 39

BROWN CIRCLE

Stitched on clay Linda 27 over 2
threads, the finished design size is
2⅞″ x 2⅞″. The fabric was cut 8″ x 8″.

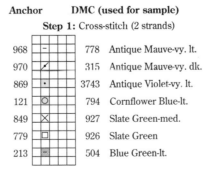

Anchor		DMC (used for sample)	
		Step 1: Cross-stitch (2 strands)	
968	−	778	Antique Mauve-vy. lt.
970	∕	315	Antique Mauve-vy. dk.
869	·	3743	Antique Violet-vy. lt.
121	O	794	Cornflower Blue-lt.
849	✕	927	Slate Green-med.
779	□	926	Slate Green
213	−	504	Blue Green-lt.

SNOWFLAKE DOLL

MATERIALS
- Patterns on page 154
- ⅛ yard of muslin
- Thread to match fabrics, gold metallic
- Scrap of cream textured-cotton yarn
- Acrylic paints: brown, blue, red, white
- Fine-point paintbrush
- Fine-point permanent black pen
- 5½″ x 15½″ piece of light green fabric
- 18″ (½″-wide) flat white lace
- 1 package (2-mm) pearl beads
- 1 package of iridescent seed beads
- 5 (½″-wide) white plastic snowflakes
- Knitting needle for stuffing tool
- Beading needle

DIRECTIONS
Patterns include ¼″ seam allowance.

1. Make body. Transfer patterns and cut out as indicated. With right sides facing, stitch body pieces together, leaving bottom edge open as indicated on pattern. Clip curves and turn. Stuff firmly, using knitting needle on arms. With right sides facing, stitch 2 leg pieces together, leaving open as indicated on pattern. Clip curves and turn. Stuff firmly, using knitting needle. Repeat for second leg. Fold bottom edge of body under ¼″ and insert open ends of legs. Topstitch opening closed, securing legs in seam.

2. Complete head. Fold yarn into 1″-long loops and tack to head. Referring to Diagram, paint face with acrylic paints, mixing colors to achieve desired shades. Let dry. Paint a white dot on right side of each eye; then with pen make black dot in center of each eye.

3. Make dress. With right sides facing and raw edges aligned, match ends of green fabric and stitch a 3″ seam. Press seam open. (This seam is center back of dress. Opening is neck placket.) Fold raw edges of placket under ¼″ and press. To hem dress, fold bottom edge under ¼″ and then ½″. Press. Topstitch close to first fold. Topstitch lace to right side of dress ½″ above hem line. Fold dress in half with seam in center back. Starting at raw edge along each side fold, cut 1 (1″-long) slash for armholes. Fold raw neck edge under ¼″ and run a gathering thread along fold, beginning and ending at center back and ignoring slashes. Place dress on doll; armholes should fit snugly. Gather neck tightly and secure at center back. Slipstitch straight edge of remaining lace along neckline, covering gathers.

4. Embellish doll. Using white thread, string 1 (4″) length of pearl beads, tie thread ends, and tack in a circle around top of head for crown. Using white thread, string 1 (8″) length of seed beads with 1 snowflake in center. Secure ends at center back of neck for necklace. String 1 (4″) length of seed beads and attach 1 snowflake to each end; tack to 1 hand. Sew 2 snowflakes and several seed beads to dress front above lace as desired (see photo). For hanger, sew a 9″ piece of gold metallic thread through top of doll and knot ends together to make a loop.

Diagram

DECORATIVE BOWL AND BALLS

MATERIALS (for bowl and 6 balls)
- Fingering-weight mercerized cotton (184-yd. ball): 2 claret for bowl; 1 each ecru, peach, mauve, purple, khaki, and gray for balls
- Size 10 steel crochet hook (or size to obtain gauge)
- 6 (3″-diameter) craft foam balls
- Assorted glass, ceramic, and wooden beads
- Assorted shank buttons
- Sewing threads to match crochet

DIRECTIONS
Gauge: 15 sts and 13 rows = 2″.
Note: Crochet abbreviations are on page 160.

1. Crochet bowl. With claret, ch 2. (*Note:* Work in bk lps only in a spiral. Use a safety pin to mark the beg of ea rnd.) *Rnd 1:* Work 6 sc in 2nd ch from hook. *Rnd 2:* Work 2 sc in ea sc around = 12 sc. *Rnd 3:* * Sc in next sc, 2 sc in next sc, rep from * around = 18 sc. *Rnd 4:* * Sc in ea of next 2 sc, 2 sc in next sc, rep from * around = 24 sc. *Rnd 5:* * Sc in ea of next 3 sc, 2 sc in next sc, rep from * around = 30 sc. *Rnd 6:* * Sc in ea of next 2 sc, 2 sc in next sc, rep from * around = 40 sc. *Rnd 7:* Rep rnd 5 = 50 sc. *Rnd 8:* * Sc in ea of next 4 sc, 2 sc in next sc = 60 sc. *Rnd 9:* Rep rnd 8 = 72 sc. *Rnd 10:* Rep rnd 8, end with sc in ea of 2 sc = 86 sc. *Rnd 11:* Sc in ea of next 2 sc, 2 sc in next sc, (sc in ea of next 6 sc, 2 sc in next sc) 11 times, sc in ea of 6 sc = 98 sc. *Rnd 12:* Work (2 sc in next sc, sc in ea of next 8 sc) 10 times, 2 sc in next sc, sc in ea of 7 sc = 109 sc. *Rnd 13:* Sc in next sc, (2 sc in next sc, sc in ea of next 8 sc) 12 times = 121 sc. *Rnds 14–15:* Work * 2 sc in next sc, sc in ea of next 10 sc, rep from * around = 144 sc after rnd 15. *Rnd 16:* Work (2 sc in next sc, sc in ea of next 14 sc) 9 times, 2 sc in next sc, sc in ea of 8 sc = 154 sc. *Rnd 17:* Sc in ea of next 6 sc, (2 sc in next sc, sc in ea of next 17 sc) 8 times, 2 sc in next sc, sc in ea of 3 sc = 163 sc. *Rnd 18:* Sc in ea of next 14 sc, (2 sc in next sc, sc in ea of next 17 sc) 8 times, 2 sc in next sc, sc in ea of 4 sc = 172 sc. *Rnd 19:* Sc in ea of next 15 sc, (2 sc in next sc, sc in ea of next 19 sc) 7 times, 2 sc in next sc, sc in ea of 16 sc = 180 sc. *Rnd 20:* Sc in ea of next 3 sc, (2 sc in next sc, sc in ea of next 24 sc) 7 times, 2 sc in next sc, sc in last sc = 188 sc. *Rnd 21:* Sc in ea of next 23 sc, (2 sc in next sc, sc in ea of next 24 sc) 6 times, 2 sc in next sc, sc in ea of 14 sc = 195 sc. *Rnd 22:* Sc in ea of next 15 sc, * 2 sc in next sc, sc in ea of next 29 sc, rep from * around = 201 sc. *Rnd 23:* Work (2 sc in next sc, sc in ea of next 34 sc) 5 times, 2 sc in next sc, sc in ea of 25 sc = 207 sc. *Rnd 24:* Sc in ea of next 4 sc, (2 sc in next sc, sc in ea of next 39 sc) 5 times, sc in ea of 3 sc = 212 sc. *Rnd 25:* Sc in ea of next 12 sc, (2 sc in next sc, sc in ea of next 44 sc) 4 times, sc in ea of 20 sc = 216 sc. *Rnd 26:* Sc in ea of next 10 sc, (2 sc in next sc, sc in ea of next 49 sc) 4 times, sc in ea of 6 sc = 220 sc. *Rnd 27:* Sc in ea of next 20 sc, * 2 sc in next sc, sc in ea of next 49 sc, rep from * around = 224 sc. *Rnd 28:* Work (2 sc in next sc, sc in ea of next 49 sc) 4 times, sc in ea of 24 sc = 228 sc. *Rnd 29:* Sc in ea of next 28 sc, * 2 sc in next sc, sc in ea of next 49 sc, rep from * around = 232 sc. *Rnd 30:* Sc in ea sc around. *Rnd 31:* * Pull up a lp in ea of next 2 sc, yo and pull through all lps on hook (dec made), sc in ea of next 9 sc, rep from * 19 times more, sc in ea of 12 sc = 212 sc. Work even for 3¼″. Fasten off. Fold down top 1½″ of basket for rim.

2. Crochet ball. (Make 1 from ea rem color.) Ch 6, join with a sl st to form a ring. (*Note:* Work in bk lps only in a spiral. Use a safety pin to mark the beg of ea rnd.) *Rnd 1:* Ch 1, 2 sc in ea st around. *Rnd 2:* (Sc in ea of next 2 sts, 2 sc in next st) around = 16 sts. *Rnd 3:* Sc in next st, (2 sc in next st, sc in ea of next 3 sts) around, end with sc in ea of 2 sts. *Rnd 4:* Work (2 sc in next st, sc in ea of next 4 sts) around = 24 sts. *Rnd 5:* Sc in ea of next 3 sts, (2 sc in next st, sc in ea of next 5 sts) around, end with sc in ea of 2 sts. *Rnd 6:* Work (2 sc in next st, sc in ea of next 6 sts) around = 32 sts. *Rnds 7–11:* Rep rnd 6. *Rnd 12:* Sc in ea of next 6 sts, (2 sc in next st, sc in ea of 3 sts) around, end with sc in ea of 4 sts = 82 sts. Work even for 1″. Slip craft foam ball inside crochet and work rnds 1–12, beg with rnd 12 and reversing shaping. Work a dec instead of ea inc as foll: pull up a lp in ea of next 2 sts, yo and through all lps on hook. When 6 sts rem, sl st 2 sts tog around. Fasten off.

3. Embellish balls. Decorate balls with beads, buttons, and decorative stitches as desired.

WOODCUTTER SANTA

MATERIALS
- Pattern on page 156
- 4" x 6" piece of ½" pine
- Scroll saw
- Electric drill with ⅟₁₆" bit
- Sandpaper: medium, fine
- Water-base wood sealer
- Acrylic paints: black, white, gold, pink, red, dark red, green, dark green, dark brown
- Paintbrushes: small flat, detail
- Modeling paste
- Palette knife
- Toothbrush
- Clear sealer
- 3" square of burlap
- 7 (4½") twigs
- Hot glue-gun and glue stick
- 19" piece of twine

DIRECTIONS
1. Prepare materials. Transfer pattern to pine and cut out. Drill 2 holes as indicated on pattern. Sand smooth. Apply wood sealer and let dry.

2. Paint ornament. Paint front and sides of Santa according to pattern. Paint eyes black and then dot with white. Referring to pattern for placement, paint dots on hatband and trim on pockets and sleeves with gold. Add "S" strokes with gold between dots on hat. Outline and shade coat with dark green. Let dry. Outline and shade hat, mittens, and boots with dark red. With palette knife, apply a thin coat of modeling paste on pompom, hair, and beard. Spread and sculpt paste for texture. Let dry. Paint pom-pom, hair, and beard with white. Let dry.

3. Antique ornament. Dilute dark brown paint with water until very thin. Load flat brush with thinned paint and lightly brush over ornament. Wipe off with a soft, lint-free cloth. Let dry. Dip bristles of toothbrush in white paint and lightly spatter ornament. Let dry. Coat ornament with clear sealer and let dry.

4. Complete ornament. To make bundle, wrap burlap around twigs and glue in place. Glue bundle horizontally to back of Santa just above holes. Cut 2 (7") pieces of twine. Thread 1 piece of twine through each hole. Tie around bundle in back. For hanger, fold remaining twine in half. Glue ends to back of Santa above bundle.

Woodcutter Santa would love to play a part in your tabletop decorations. Just leave off his hanger and stand him in front of a small wooden bowl full of shiny red apples sprinkled with greenery.

PIECED WREATH

MATERIALS
- Pattern on page 156
- Fabric scraps: light green, dark green, cranberry, burgundy
- Scrap of fleece
- 5" square of foam-core board
- Thread to match fabrics
- 6" square of fusible web
- Craft glue
- 2 (¼") cranberry heart-shaped buttons
- 1 yard (⅛"-wide) burgundy satin ribbon
- (3-mm) green glass beads

DIRECTIONS
All seams are ¼".

1. Prepare materials. Cut 1 (6") square from light green fabric and set aside. Transfer wreath pattern to another scrap of light green fabric, adding ¼" seam allowance to outer edge, and cut 1 along outer edge of pattern only. Transfer wreath pattern to fleece and cut 1 along outer edge of pattern only. Transfer wreath pattern to foam-core board and cut 1 along outer and inner edges. Cut dark green, cranberry, and burgundy fabrics into 10"-long strips, in widths varying from ¾" to ½".

2. Make wreath front. With right sides facing, raw edges aligned, and alternating colors, sew long edges of strips together to make 1 striped piece. Trim seams to ⅛". Cutting across seams, cut striped piece into 4 (2½") pieces. With right sides facing, raw edges aligned, and alternating direction of stripes, arrange as shown in photo and sew 4 pieces together to make a square. Center and transfer wreath pattern to striped fabric and cut 1 along outer and inner edges.

3. Complete ornament. With right sides up and fusible web between, center wreath front on green fabric square. Fuse according to manufacturer's instructions. Trim green fabric 1" from outer edge of wreath front. With burgundy thread, machine-satin-stitch around outer and inner edges of wreath front. Glue fleece circle to foam-core wreath. Place wreath front right side up over fleece/foam-core wreath, wrap edges to back of foam-core, and glue. Fold under seam allowance along edges of light green fabric circle. With wrong sides facing, center and glue green fabric circle to back of wreath. Let dry.

4. Embellish ornament. With matching thread, sew heart-shaped buttons in center of wreath. For hanger, cut 1 (10") length of ribbon. Fold ribbon in half. Knot ribbon 3" from fold. Knot ends. Tack ends to top center of ornament back. Fold remaining ribbon into 1–1½" loops. Referring to photo, tack ribbon loops to bottom front of wreath. Tack beads to wreath in 3 groups of 3 each, placing 1 group over tacked ribbons.

Hang this festive wreath around the neck of a bottle of wine or herb vinegar—you'll have a gift that's twice the fun!

FOLK DOLL

MATERIALS
- Patterns on page 158
- Fabric scraps: muslin, navy check, red check
- 4″ square of cream print for scarf
- Thread to match muslin
- ½ yard (⅛″-wide) cream satin ribbon
- Small amount of stuffing
- Monofilament

DIRECTIONS
Patterns include ¼″ seam allowance.

1. Prepare materials. Transfer patterns and cut out as indicated. Unravel threads on all edges of cream print to make ⅛″ fringe.

2. Make doll. With right sides facing and raw edges aligned, stitch body pieces together, leaving an opening as indicated on pattern. Turn and stuff lightly. Slipstitch opening closed. To define arms and legs, topstitch through all layers as indicated on pattern.

3. Make clothing. With right sides facing and raw edges aligned, stitch sides of petticoat pieces together. Turn under ¼″ on bottom edge and hem. Turn under ¼″ around edge of waist and run a gathering thread close to fold. Slip petticoat on doll, placing hem just above feet, and gather to fit waist. Slipstitch waist of petticoat to doll.

For dress, with right sides facing and raw edges aligned, stitch dress pieces together along sides, underarms, and shoulders, leaving neck and sleeves open as indicated on pattern. Turn under ½″ on bottom edge and hem. Turn edges of neck and sleeves under ¼″ and run a gathering thread close to fold. Place dress on doll, gather neck and wrist threads, and secure. Fold cream print scarf in half diagonally, making a triangle. Place scarf over doll's shoulders, overlapping in center front at waist, and tack ends to doll.

4. Complete ornament. Tie ribbon in bow around doll's waist; knot ribbon ends. For hanger, stitch an 8″ length of monofilament through top back of doll's head and knot ends together to make a loop.

MUSLIN SHEEP

MATERIALS (for 1)
- Patterns on page 156–157
- Dressmaker's pen
- Scrap of muslin
- Thread to match
- Scrap of white canvas for base
- Stuffing
- Scrap of foam-core board
- Hot-glue gun and glue sticks
- Acrylic paints: see patterns
- Assorted paintbrushes
- 1 package of crepe hair: **For ram:** white; **for ewe:** black
- 20″ (⅜″-wide) pink grosgrain ribbon

DIRECTIONS
Patterns include ¼″ seam allowance.

1. Prepare materials. For each: Using dressmaker's pen, transfer patterns and details for desired sheep and base and cut out as indicated.

2. Make sheep. For ewe: Using a narrow zigzag, machine-satin-stitch around each ear. **For each:** With right sides facing and raw edges aligned, stitch body pieces together, leaving bottom edge open. Turn and stuff firmly to within ½″ of bottom edge. Insert foam-core base. Fold bottom edges of muslin ¼″ over foam core and glue. Glue canvas base to foam-core base.

3. Paint sheep. For each: Referring to pattern and photo, paint both sides of sheep as desired. Let dry.

4. Complete sheep. For ewe: Referring to pattern, glue ears to head. **For each:** Separate crepe hair and glue to body and head, leaving face uncovered. Fluff crepe hair slightly. Tie ribbon in a bow around neck.

TINY EMBROIDERED PILLOWS

MATERIALS (for 1)
- Patterns on page 158
- 5″ square of muslin
- Embroidery floss: see color key
- Embroidery needle
- Dressmaker's pen
- 4″ x 8″ piece of dark rose fabric
- Scrap of mauve fabric
- Scrap of burgundy fabric
- Thread to match fabrics
- Small amount of stuffing
- ¼ yard (⅜″-wide) white satin ribbon
- 2 (8-mm) wooden beads

DIRECTIONS
Patterns include ¼″ seam allowance.

1. Embroider design. Center and work embroidery design on muslin square (see Diagram A or B). Straight lines indicate direction of stitches. With design centered, trim design piece to 2″ x 2″.

2. Prepare materials. Transfer pillow pattern to dark rose fabric and cut 2. For ornament with laurel center, transfer corner pattern to mauve fabric and cut 4. For ornament with medallion center, transfer corner pattern and cut 2 from mauve and 2 from burgundy fabric.

3. Assemble ornament front. Fold seam allowance under on all edges of design piece. Center and slipstitch design piece to right side of 1 dark rose pillow piece (see pillow pattern). With right sides facing and raw edges aligned, stitch 1 short edge only of 2 corner pieces together as indicated on pattern. Repeat to add remaining 2 corner pieces to make a 4-corner unit. Press seams open. With right sides up and raw edges aligned, place corner unit on top of design piece. Fold seam allowance under on inside straight edges of corner unit. Using a running stitch and stitching close to straight edges, stitch corner unit to design piece.

4. Complete ornament. With right sides facing, raw edges aligned, and leaving a small opening on 1 side, stitch ornament front to back. Sew a running stitch in seam allowance of 1 corner; gather thread slightly and secure. Repeat for other 3 corners. Turn and stuff. Slipstitch opening closed. For hanger, fold ribbon in half and thread ends through beads. Knot ribbon ends together to make a loop and tack knot to back of ornament.

Stitch Key
1—Satin stitch
2—Stemstitch

Color Key
(*Note:* Numbers are for DMC floss.)
A—807 Peacock Blue
B—797 Royal Blue
C—954 Nile Green
D—895 Christmas Green-dk.
E—315 Antique Mauve-vy. dk.

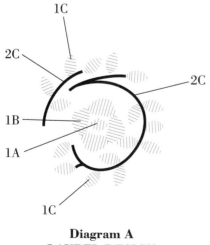

Diagram A
LAUREL DESIGN

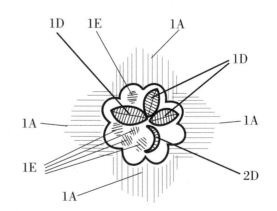

Diagram B
MEDALLION DESIGN

PATTERNS
All patterns are full-size.

WE THREE KINGS
Instructions are on page 16.

HAT
Cut 1 from velvet.

Face placement

Place on fold.

BODY
Cut 2 from velveteen
for each wise man.

FACE
Cut 1 from muslin for
each wise man.

SANTA'S FACE
Instructions are on page 26.

Leave open.

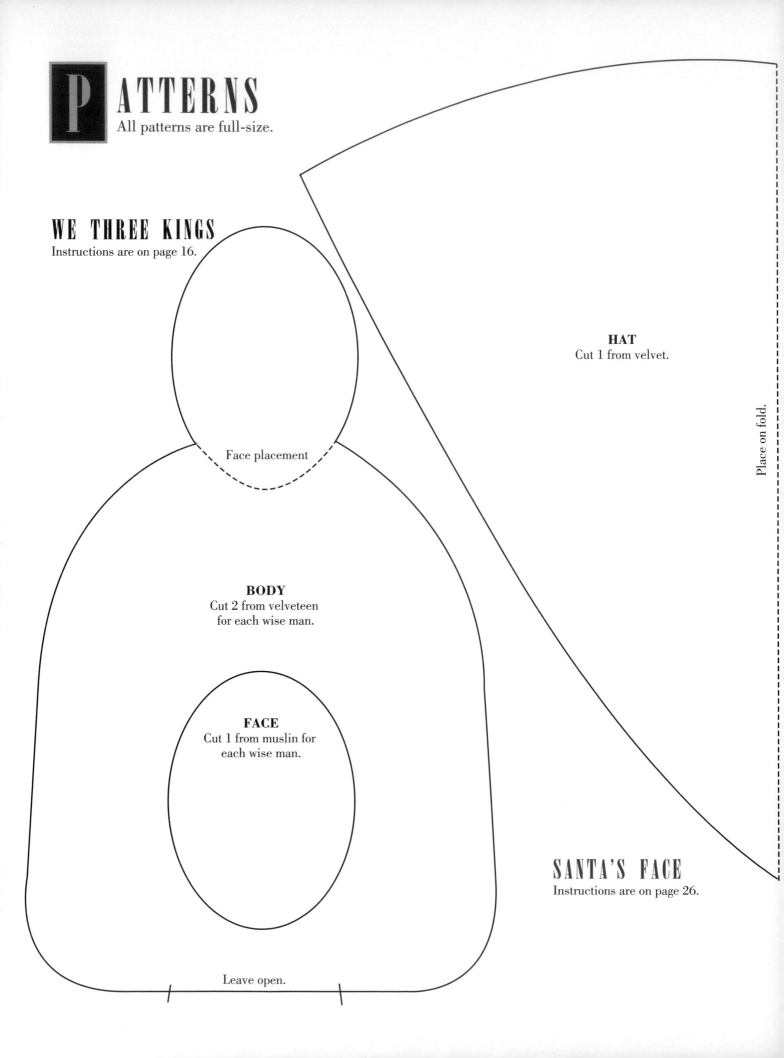

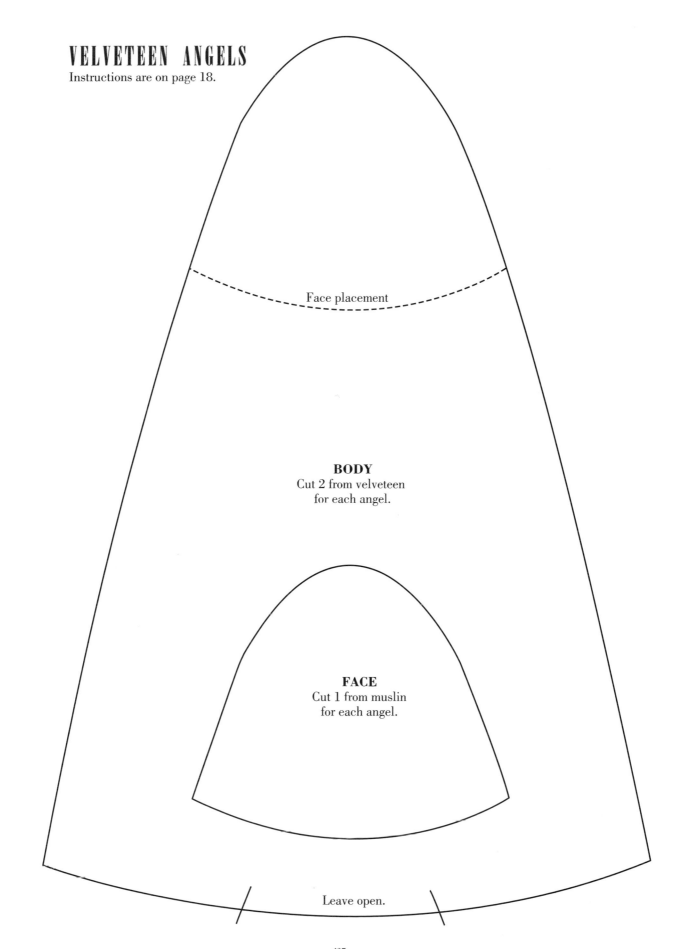

VELVETEEN ANGELS
Instructions are on page 18.

Face placement

BODY
Cut 2 from velveteen
for each angel.

FACE
Cut 1 from muslin
for each angel.

Leave open.

COWBOY SANTA

Instructions are on page 35.

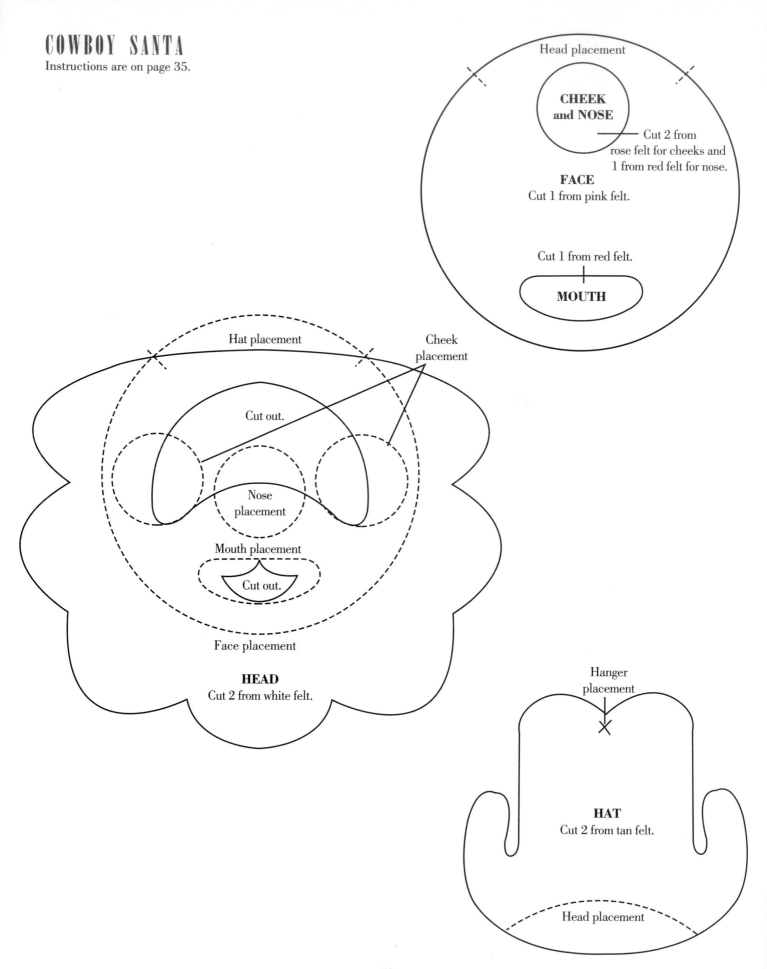

Head placement

CHEEK and NOSE

Cut 2 from rose felt for cheeks and 1 from red felt for nose.

FACE
Cut 1 from pink felt.

Cut 1 from red felt.

MOUTH

Hat placement

Cheek placement

Cut out.

Nose placement

Mouth placement

Cut out.

Face placement

HEAD
Cut 2 from white felt.

Hanger placement

HAT
Cut 2 from tan felt.

Head placement

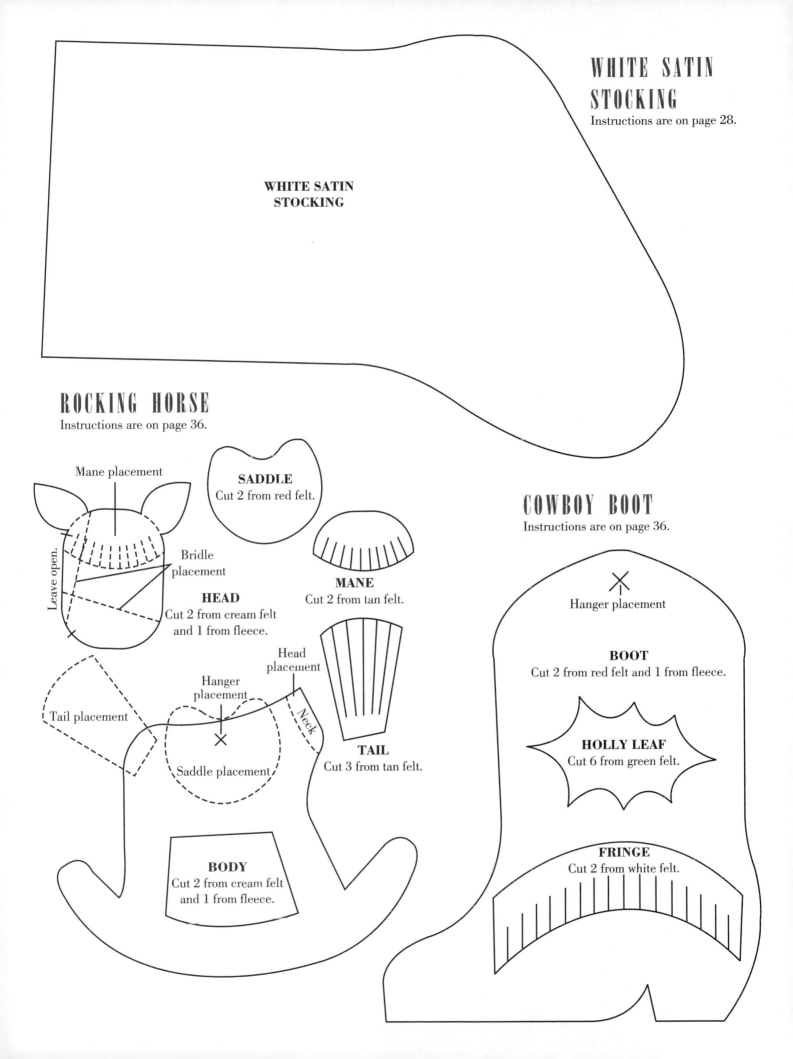

WHITE SATIN STOCKING

Instructions are on page 28.

WHITE SATIN
STOCKING

ROCKING HORSE

Instructions are on page 36.

Mane placement

Leave open.

Bridle
placement

HEAD
Cut 2 from cream felt
and 1 from fleece.

Tail placement

Hanger
placement

Saddle placement

Head
placement

Neck

BODY
Cut 2 from cream felt
and 1 from fleece.

SADDLE
Cut 2 from red felt.

MANE
Cut 2 from tan felt.

TAIL
Cut 3 from tan felt.

COWBOY BOOT

Instructions are on page 36.

Hanger placement

BOOT
Cut 2 from red felt and 1 from fleece.

HOLLY LEAF
Cut 6 from green felt.

FRINGE
Cut 2 from white felt.

COWBOY HAT
Instructions are on page 36.

HATBAND
Cut 2 from red felt.

Place on fold.

× Hanger placement

Hatband placement

HAT
Cut 2 from gold felt and 1 from fleece.

HOLLY LEAF
Cut 3 from red felt.

KNITTED SOLDIERS
Instructions are on page 42.

HAT TOP
Cut 1 from black satin for each soldier.

Place on fold.

HAT BRIM
Cut 2 from black satin for each soldier.

Place on fold.

ANTIQUE HEARTS
Instructions are on page 38.

HEART

Reverse along broken line for complete pattern.

RIBBON DOVE AND HEART
Instructions are on page 44.

HEART

Place on fold.

DOVE

SANTA AND SOLDIER NUTCRACKERS
Instructions are on page 46.

BASE
Cut 1 for each.

Side edge

Side edge

SOLDIER'S HAT
Cut 4.

PAINTED SANTA CONES
Instructions are on page 53.

LARGE BASE
Cut 1 each from foam core and canvas.

SMALL BASE
Cut 1 each from foam
core and canvas.

139

Continued on following page.

PAINTED SANTA CONES
(Continued)

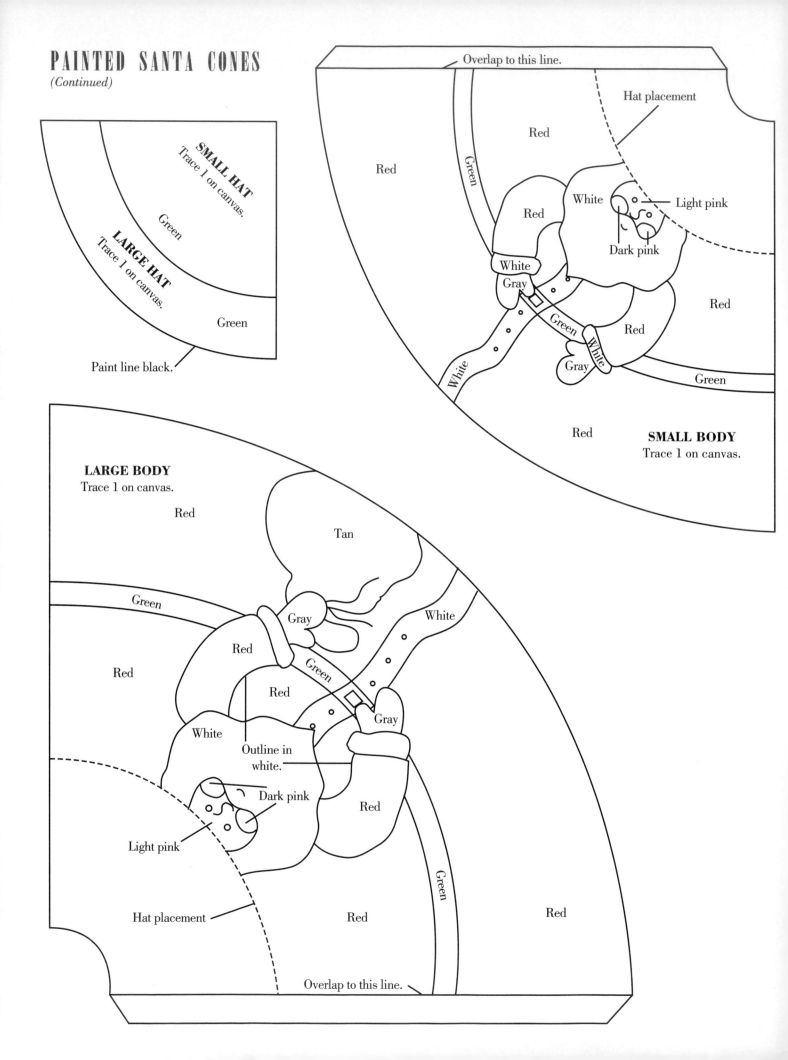

SMALL HAT
Trace 1 on canvas.

Green

LARGE HAT
Trace 1 on canvas.

Green

Green

Paint line black.

Overlap to this line.

Hat placement

Red

Red

Green

Red

White

Light pink

Dark pink

White

Gray

Red

Red

Green

White

White

Gray

Green

Red

Red

SMALL BODY
Trace 1 on canvas.

LARGE BODY
Trace 1 on canvas.

Red

Tan

Green

Gray

White

Red

Red

Red

Green

White

Gray

Outline in white.

Dark pink

Red

Light pink

Hat placement

Green

Red

Red

Overlap to this line.

JOLLY JESTERS
Instructions are on page 54.

ARM
Cut 1 from each fabric.

Place on fold.

Place on fold.

HAT
Cut 1 from desired fabric.

A

B

BODY
Cut 1 from each fabric.

Place on fold.

WOODLAND ORNAMENTS
Instructions are on page 58.

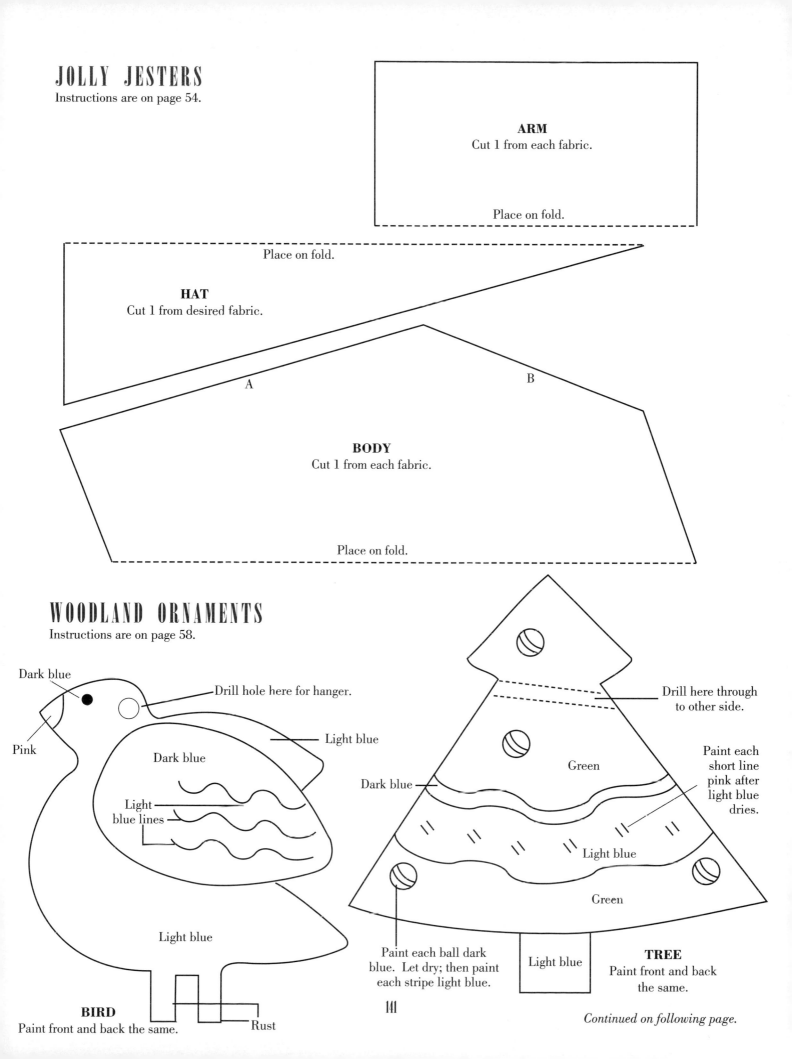

Dark blue

Drill hole here for hanger.

Pink

Light blue

Dark blue

Light
blue lines

Light blue

Drill here through
to other side.

Paint each
short line
pink after
light blue
dries.

Green

Dark blue

Light blue

Green

BIRD
Paint front and back the same.

Rust

Paint each ball dark
blue. Let dry; then paint
each stripe light blue.

Light blue

TREE
Paint front and back
the same.

141

Continued on following page.

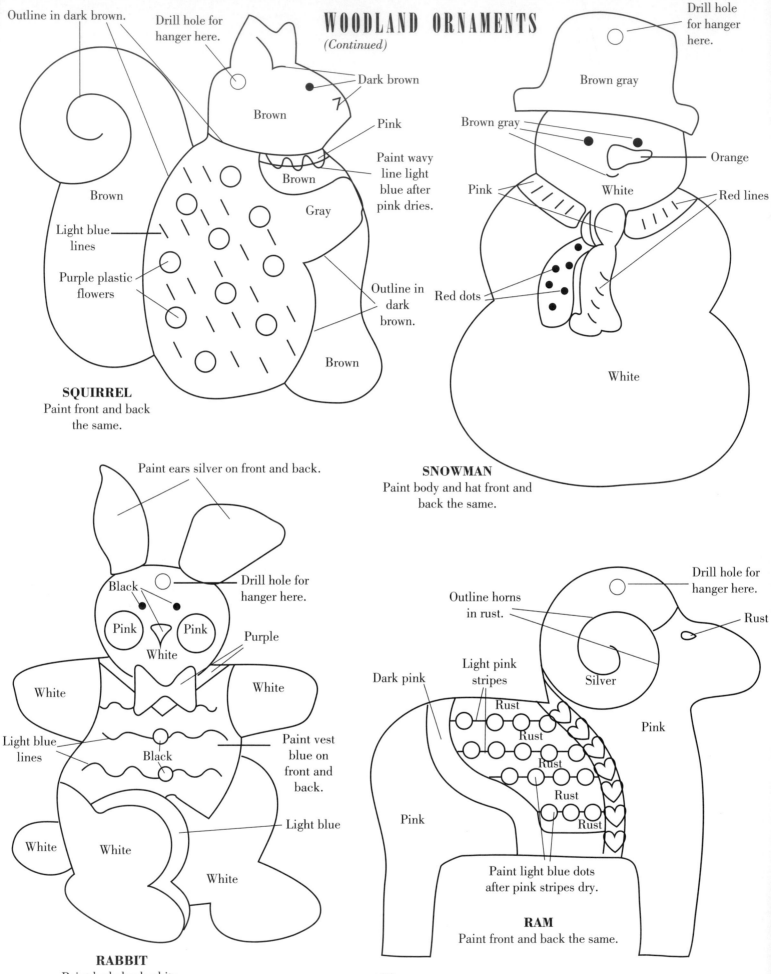

Outline in dark brown.

Drill hole for hanger here.

Dark brown

Brown

Pink

Paint wavy line light blue after pink dries.

Brown

Brown

Gray

Brown

Light blue lines

Purple plastic flowers

Outline in dark brown.

Brown

SQUIRREL
Paint front and back the same.

Drill hole for hanger here.

Brown gray

Brown gray

Orange

Pink

White

Red lines

Red dots

White

SNOWMAN
Paint body and hat front and back the same.

Paint ears silver on front and back.

Black

Pink

Pink

White

Purple

White

White

Light blue lines

Black

Paint vest blue on front and back.

Light blue

White

White

White

RABBIT
Paint body back white.

Outline horns in rust.

Drill hole for hanger here.

Rust

Light pink stripes

Silver

Dark pink

Rust

Pink

Rust

Rust

Rust

Pink

Rust

Paint light blue dots after pink stripes dry.

RAM
Paint front and back the same.

142

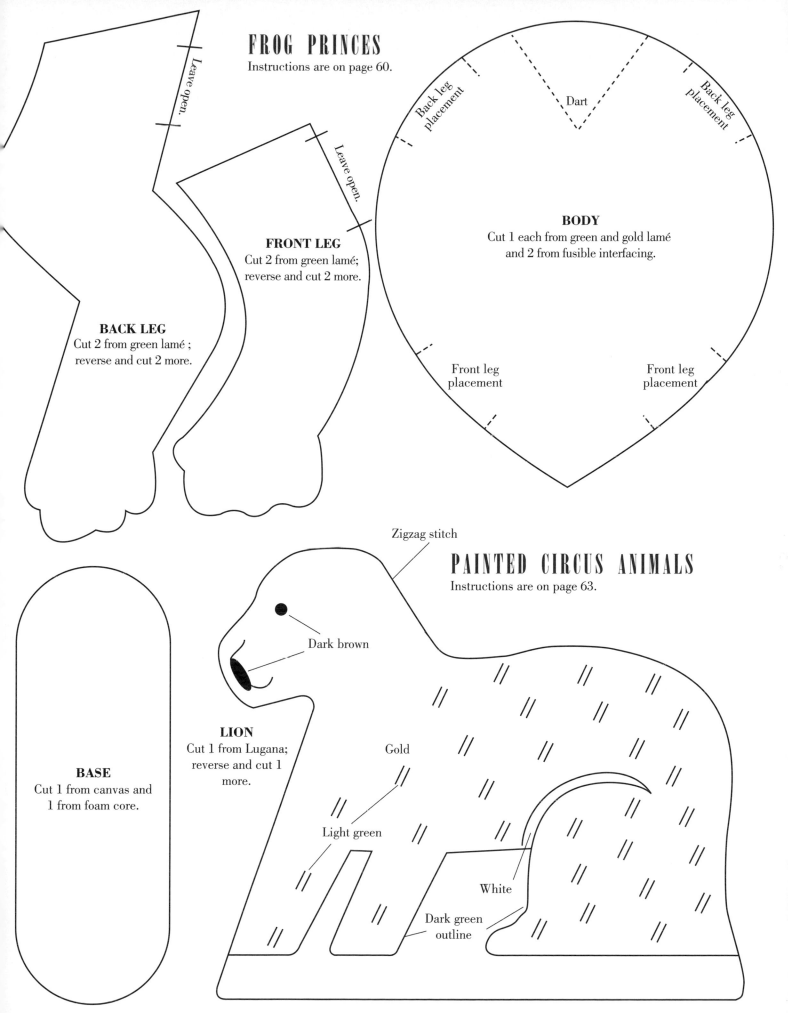

FROG PRINCES
Instructions are on page 60.

Leave open.

Leave open.

BACK LEG
Cut 2 from green lamé ;
reverse and cut 2 more.

FRONT LEG
Cut 2 from green lamé;
reverse and cut 2 more.

Back leg placement

Dart

Back leg placement

BODY
Cut 1 each from green and gold lamé
and 2 from fusible interfacing.

Front leg placement

Front leg placement

Zigzag stitch

PAINTED CIRCUS ANIMALS
Instructions are on page 63.

Dark brown

LION
Cut 1 from Lugana;
reverse and cut 1
more.

BASE
Cut 1 from canvas and
1 from foam core.

Gold

Light green

White

Dark green
outline

Continued on following page.

PAINTED CIRCUS ANIMALS

(Continued)

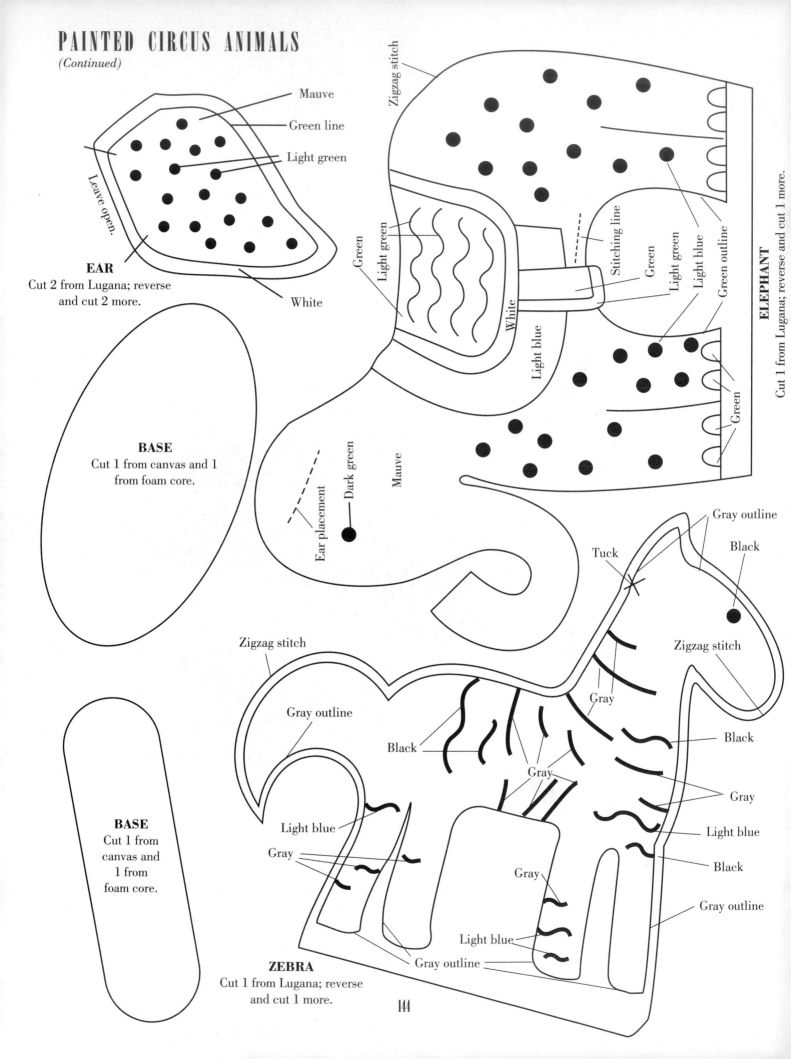

Mauve

Green line

Light green

Leave open.

EAR
Cut 2 from Lugana; reverse
and cut 2 more.

White

Zigzag stitch

Green

Light green

White

Light blue

Stitching line

Green

Light green

Light blue

Green outline

ELEPHANT
Cut 1 from Lugana; reverse and cut 1 more.

Green

BASE
Cut 1 from canvas and 1
from foam core.

Ear placement

Dark green

Mauve

Gray outline

Black

Tuck

Zigzag stitch

Gray

Zigzag stitch

Gray outline

Black

Black

Gray

Gray

Light blue

Light blue

Black

Gray

Light blue

BASE
Cut 1 from
canvas and
1 from
foam core.

Gray

Gray outline

ZEBRA
Cut 1 from Lugana; reverse
and cut 1 more.

144

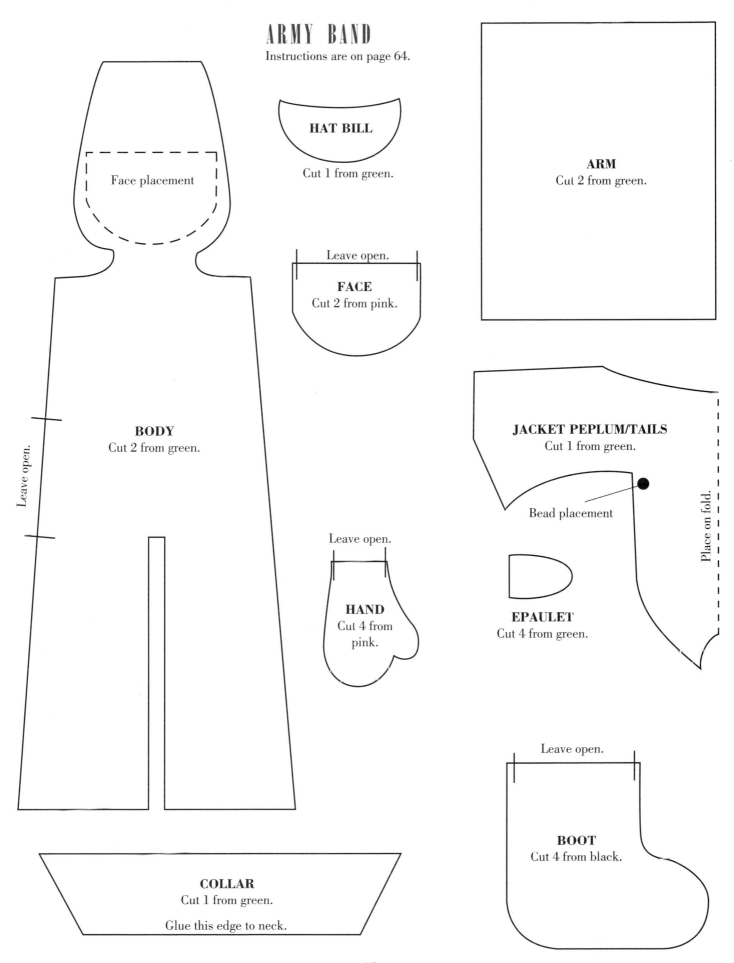

ARMY BAND

Instructions are on page 64.

HAT BILL

Cut 1 from green.

Face placement

Leave open.

FACE
Cut 2 from pink.

ARM
Cut 2 from green.

BODY
Cut 2 from green.

Leave open.

JACKET PEPLUM/TAILS
Cut 1 from green.

Bead placement

Place on fold.

Leave open.

HAND
Cut 4 from pink.

EPAULET
Cut 4 from green.

Leave open.

BOOT
Cut 4 from black.

COLLAR
Cut 1 from green.

Glue this edge to neck.

ICE CREAM CONE

Instructions are on page 68.

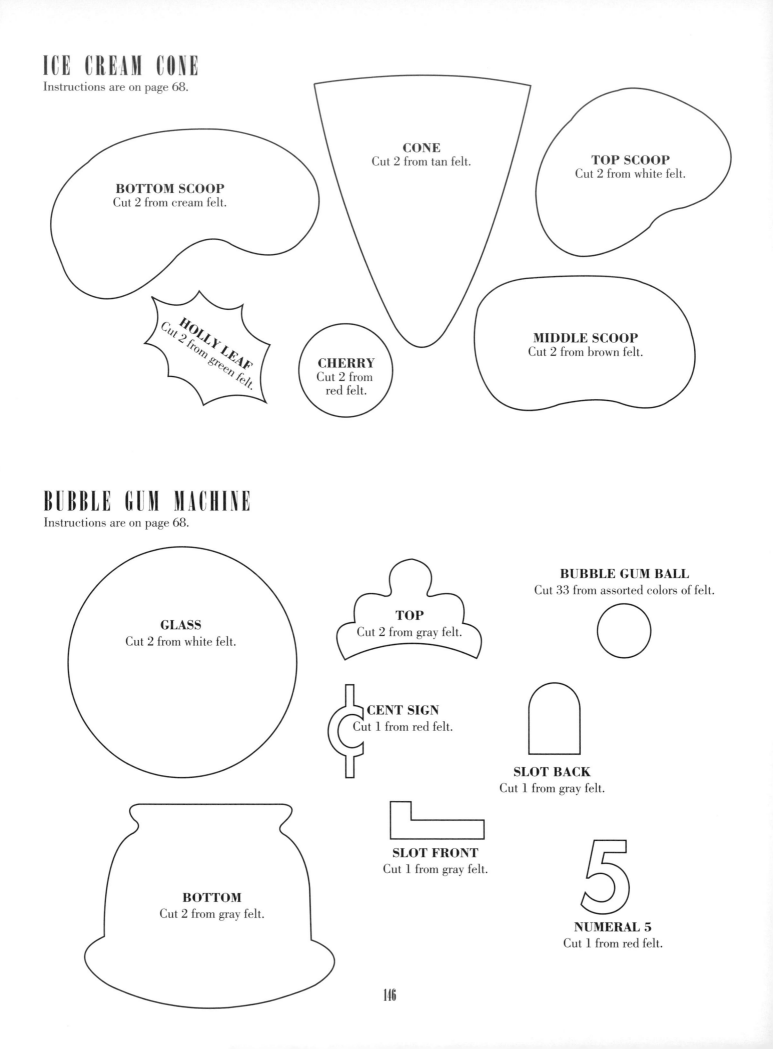

CONE
Cut 2 from tan felt.

TOP SCOOP
Cut 2 from white felt.

BOTTOM SCOOP
Cut 2 from cream felt.

HOLLY LEAF
Cut 2 from green felt.

CHERRY
Cut 2 from red felt.

MIDDLE SCOOP
Cut 2 from brown felt.

BUBBLE GUM MACHINE

Instructions are on page 68.

GLASS
Cut 2 from white felt.

TOP
Cut 2 from gray felt.

BUBBLE GUM BALL
Cut 33 from assorted colors of felt.

CENT SIGN
Cut 1 from red felt.

SLOT BACK
Cut 1 from gray felt.

SLOT FRONT
Cut 1 from gray felt.

BOTTOM
Cut 2 from gray felt.

NUMERAL 5
Cut 1 from red felt.

BRONZED TWIG ORNAMENTS
Instructions are on page 72.

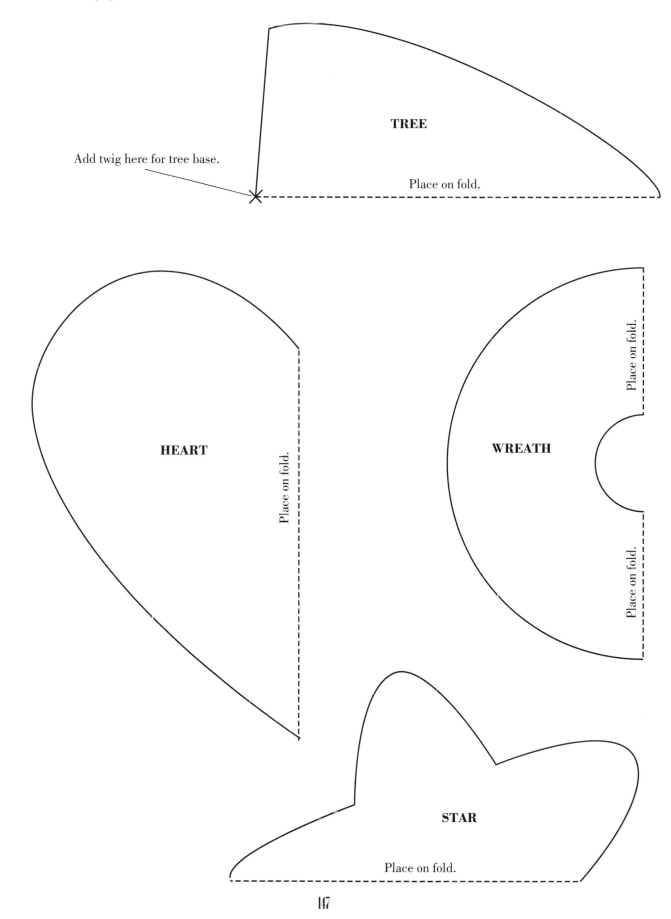

TREE

Place on fold.

Add twig here for tree base.

HEART

Place on fold.

WREATH

Place on fold.

Place on fold.

STAR

Place on fold.

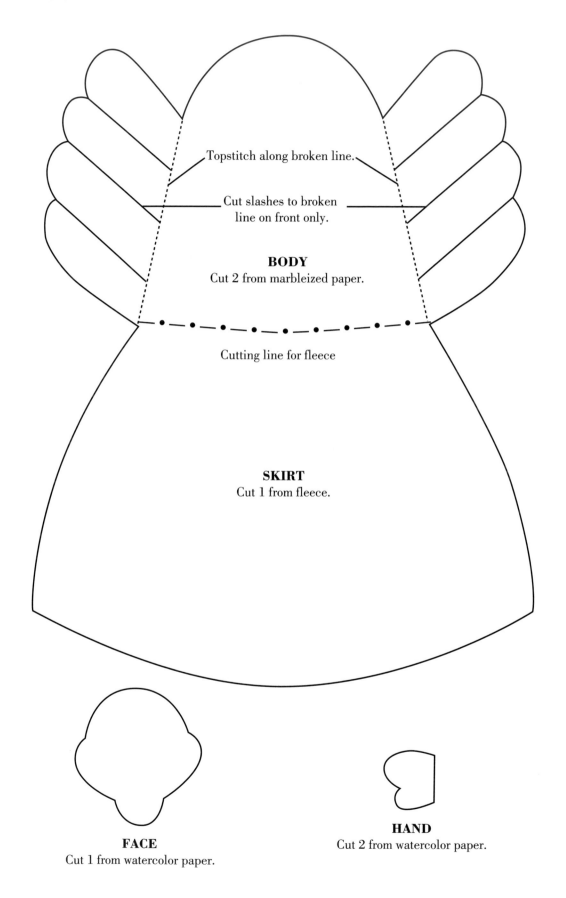

Topstitch along broken line.

Cut slashes to broken line on front only.

BODY
Cut 2 from marbleized paper.

Cutting line for fleece

SKIRT
Cut 1 from fleece.

FACE
Cut 1 from watercolor paper.

HAND
Cut 2 from watercolor paper.

RIBBON EMBROIDERY ORNAMENTS
Instructions are on page 83.

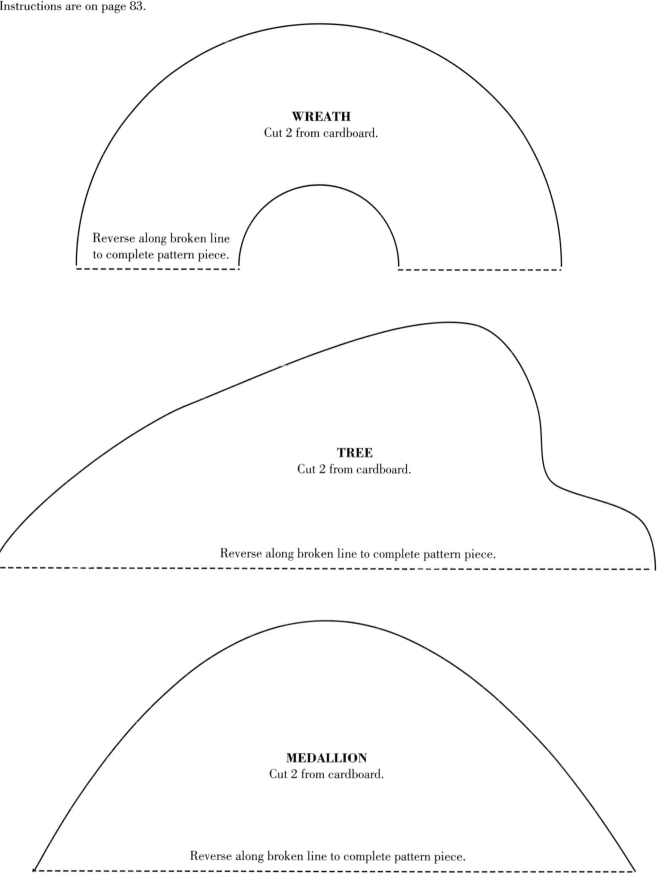

WREATH
Cut 2 from cardboard.

Reverse along broken line
to complete pattern piece.

TREE
Cut 2 from cardboard.

Reverse along broken line to complete pattern piece.

MEDALLION
Cut 2 from cardboard.

Reverse along broken line to complete pattern piece.

DIAMOND

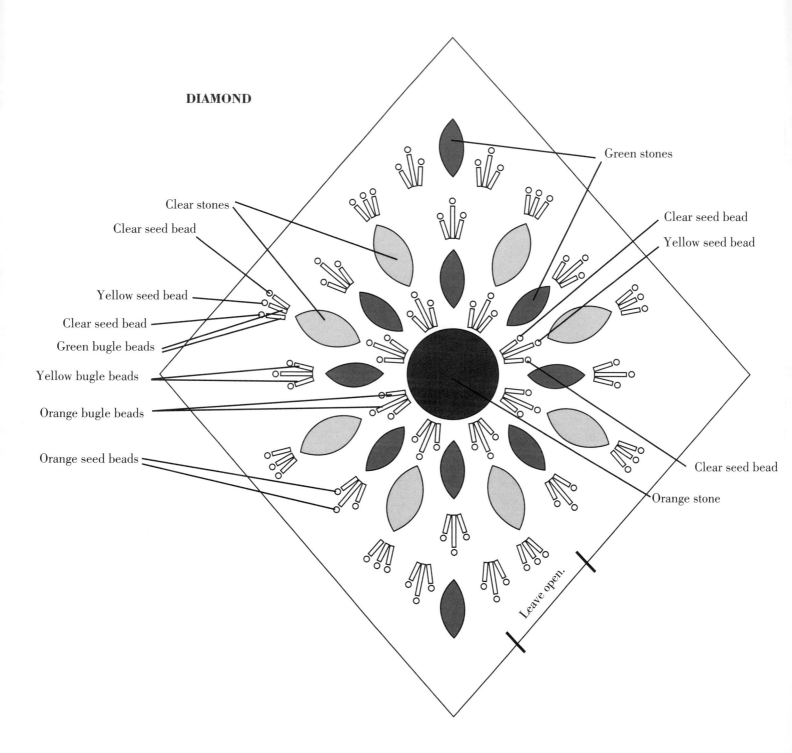

Green stones

Clear stones

Clear seed bead

Clear seed bead

Yellow seed bead

Yellow seed bead

Clear seed bead

Green bugle beads

Yellow bugle beads

Orange bugle beads

Clear seed bead

Orange stone

Orange seed beads

Leave open.

Continued on following page.

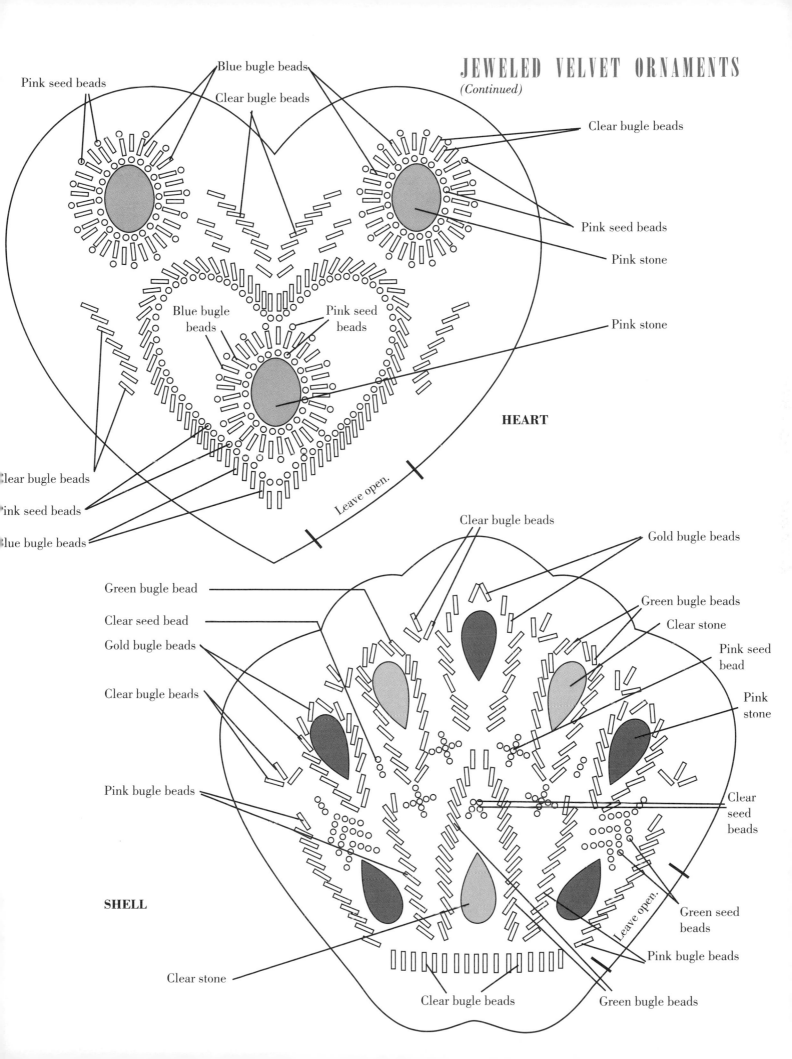

Pink seed beads

Blue bugle beads

Clear bugle beads

Clear bugle beads

Pink seed beads

Pink stone

Pink stone

Blue bugle beads

Pink seed beads

Clear bugle beads

Pink seed beads

Blue bugle beads

HEART

Leave open.

Clear bugle beads

Gold bugle beads

Green bugle bead

Green bugle beads

Clear stone

Clear seed bead

Gold bugle beads

Pink seed bead

Pink stone

Clear bugle beads

Pink bugle beads

Clear seed beads

SHELL

Green seed beads

Pink bugle beads

Clear stone

Clear bugle beads

Green bugle beads

ANIMAL DOLL
Instructions are on page 100.

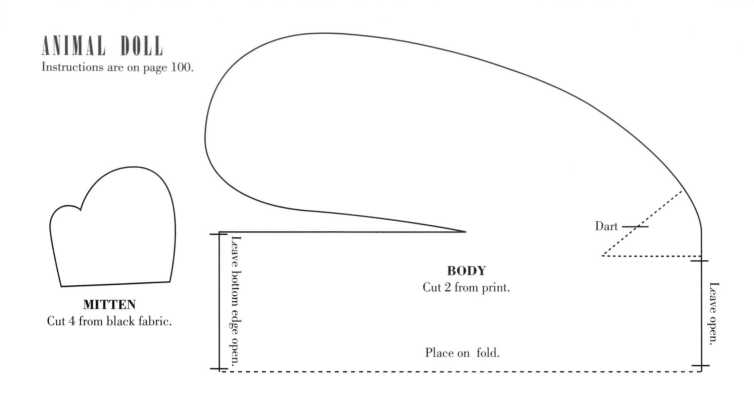

MITTEN
Cut 4 from black fabric.

BODY
Cut 2 from print.

Leave bottom edge open.

Place on fold.

Dart

Leave open.

QUILTED BASKETS
Instructions are on page 104.

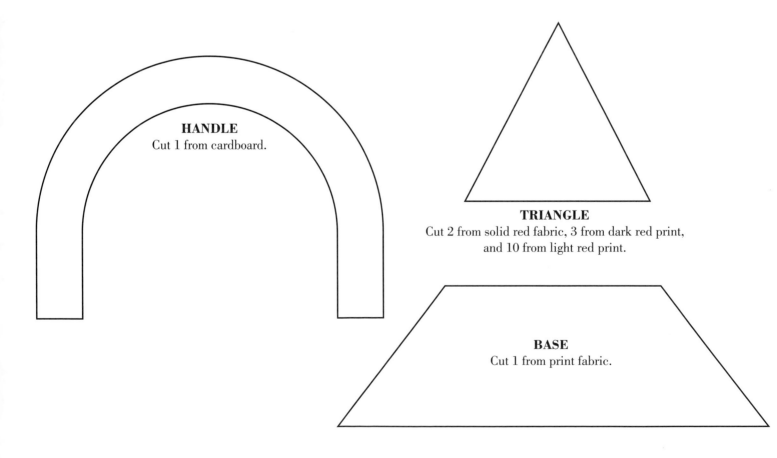

HANDLE
Cut 1 from cardboard.

TRIANGLE
Cut 2 from solid red fabric, 3 from dark red print,
and 10 from light red print.

BASE
Cut 1 from print fabric.

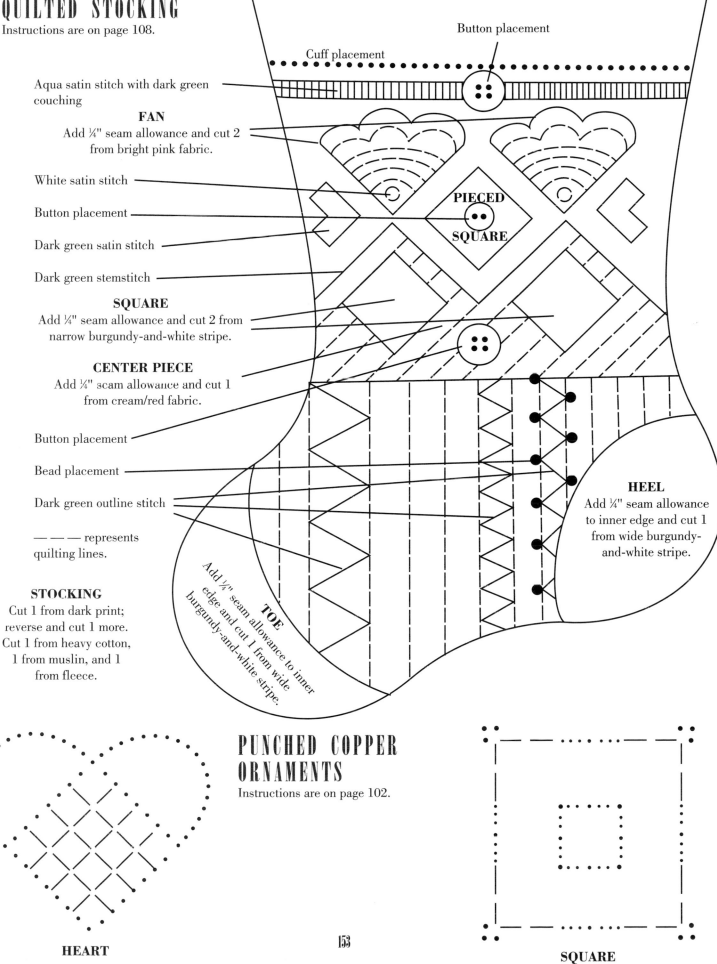

QUILTED STOCKING

Instructions are on page 108.

Aqua satin stitch with dark green couching

FAN
Add ¼" seam allowance and cut 2 from bright pink fabric.

White satin stitch

Button placement

Dark green satin stitch

Dark green stemstitch

SQUARE
Add ¼" seam allowance and cut 2 from narrow burgundy-and-white stripe.

CENTER PIECE
Add ¼" seam allowance and cut 1 from cream/red fabric.

Button placement

Bead placement

Dark green outline stitch

— — — represents quilting lines.

STOCKING
Cut 1 from dark print; reverse and cut 1 more. Cut 1 from heavy cotton, 1 from muslin, and 1 from fleece.

Cuff placement

Button placement

PIECED SQUARE

HEEL
Add ¼" seam allowance to inner edge and cut 1 from wide burgundy-and-white stripe.

TOE
Add ¼" seam allowance to inner edge and cut 1 from wide burgundy-and-white stripe.

PUNCHED COPPER ORNAMENTS

Instructions are on page 102.

HEART

SQUARE

PLEASANT PEASANTS

Instructions are on page 110.

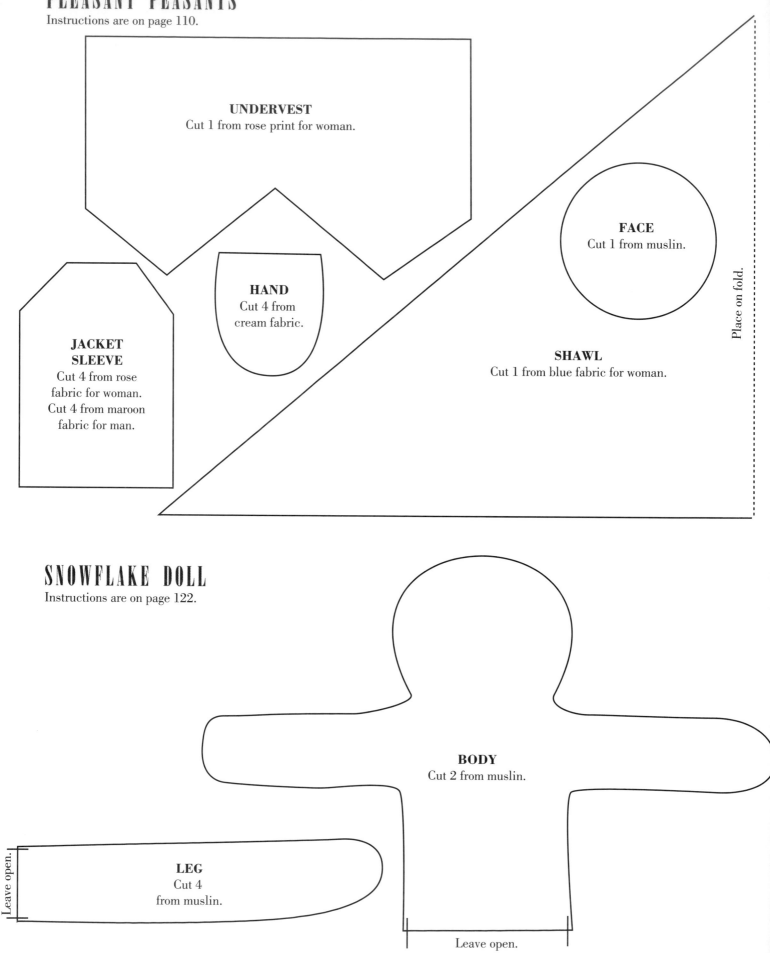

UNDERVEST
Cut 1 from rose print for woman.

FACE
Cut 1 from muslin.

HAND
Cut 4 from
cream fabric.

**JACKET
SLEEVE**
Cut 4 from rose
fabric for woman.
Cut 4 from maroon
fabric for man.

SHAWL
Cut 1 from blue fabric for woman.

Place on fold.

SNOWFLAKE DOLL

Instructions are on page 122.

BODY
Cut 2 from muslin.

LEG
Cut 4
from muslin.

Leave open.

Leave open.

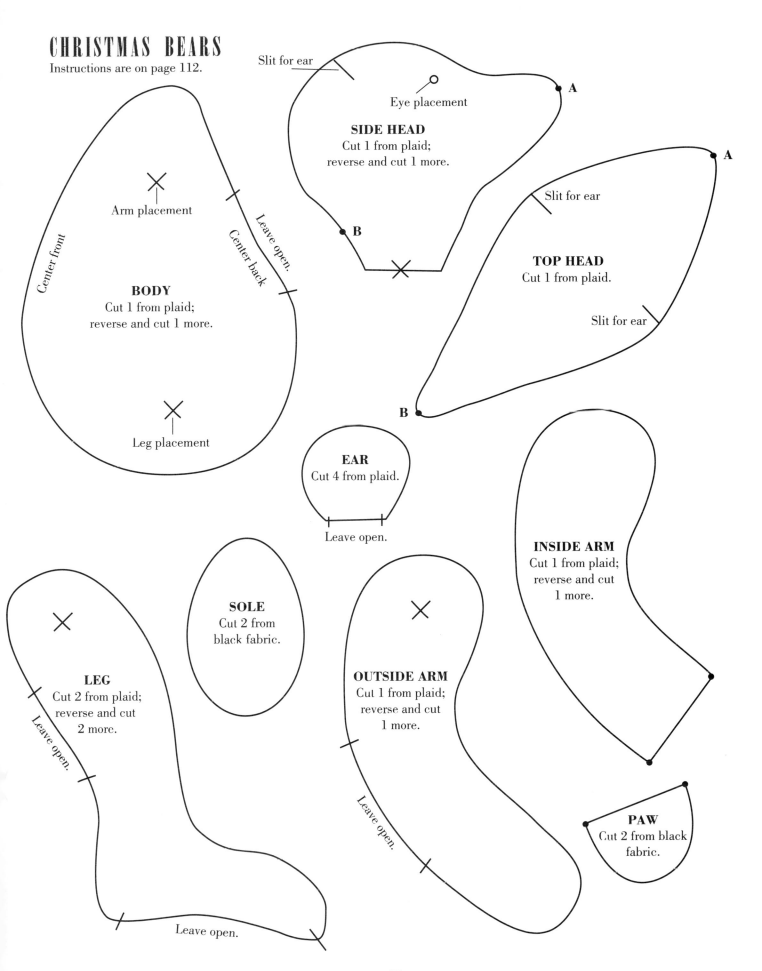

CHRISTMAS BEARS
Instructions are on page 112.

SIDE HEAD
Cut 1 from plaid;
reverse and cut 1 more.

Slit for ear

Eye placement

A

B

TOP HEAD
Cut 1 from plaid.

Slit for ear

Slit for ear

A

B

Arm placement

Center front

Center back

Leave open.

BODY
Cut 1 from plaid;
reverse and cut 1 more.

Leg placement

EAR
Cut 4 from plaid.

Leave open.

INSIDE ARM
Cut 1 from plaid;
reverse and cut
1 more.

SOLE
Cut 2 from
black fabric.

LEG
Cut 2 from plaid;
reverse and cut
2 more.

Leave open.

OUTSIDE ARM
Cut 1 from plaid;
reverse and cut
1 more.

Leave open.

PAW
Cut 2 from black
fabric.

Leave open.

155

PIECED WREATH

Instructions are on page 128.

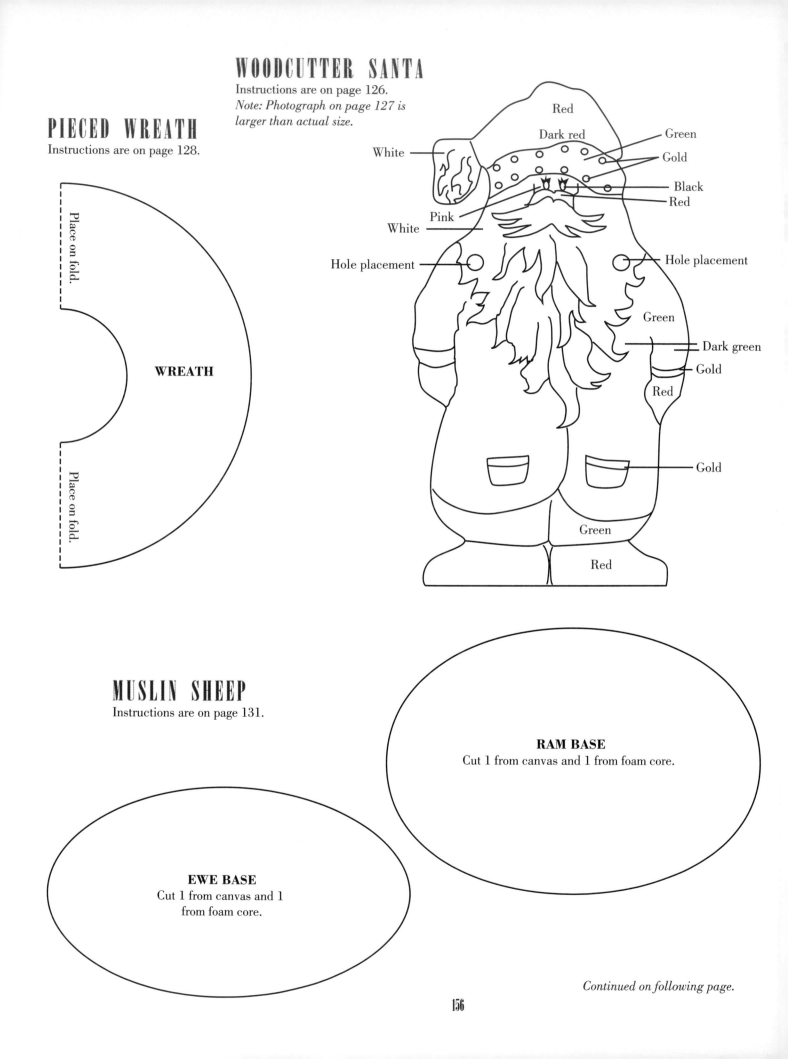

WREATH

Place on fold.

Place on fold.

WOODCUTTER SANTA

Instructions are on page 126.

Note: Photograph on page 127 is larger than actual size.

Red

Dark red

Green

Gold

White

Black

Red

Pink

White

Hole placement

Hole placement

Green

Dark green

Gold

Red

Gold

Green

Red

MUSLIN SHEEP

Instructions are on page 131.

RAM BASE
Cut 1 from canvas and 1 from foam core.

EWE BASE
Cut 1 from canvas and 1 from foam core.

Continued on following page.

MUSLIN SHEEP
(Continued)

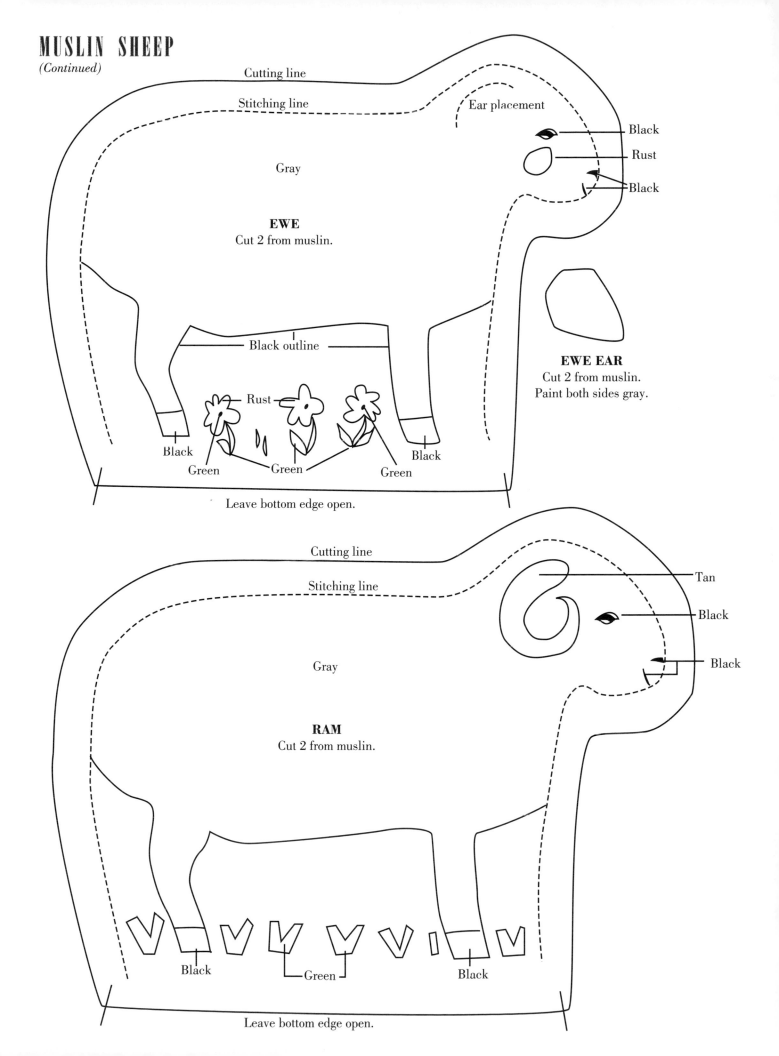

Cutting line

Stitching line

Ear placement

Black

Rust

Gray

Black

EWE
Cut 2 from muslin.

Black outline

EWE EAR
Cut 2 from muslin.
Paint both sides gray.

Rust

Black

Green

Green

Green

Black

Leave bottom edge open.

Cutting line

Stitching line

Tan

Black

Gray

Black

RAM
Cut 2 from muslin.

Black

Green

Black

Leave bottom edge open.

FOLK DOLL

Instructions are on page 130.

TINY EMBROIDERED PILLOWS

Instructions are on page 132.

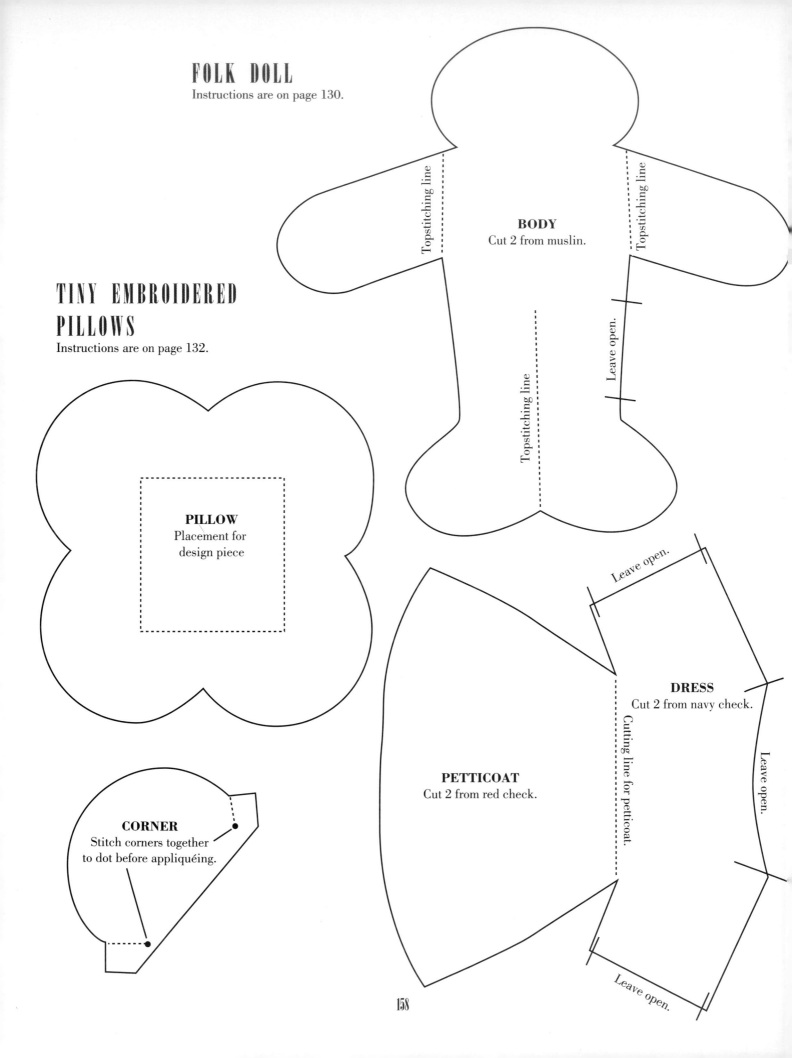

BODY
Cut 2 from muslin.

Topstitching line

Topstitching line

Topstitching line

Topstitching line

Leave open.

PILLOW
Placement for
design piece

DRESS
Cut 2 from navy check.

Leave open.

Leave open.

Cutting line for petticoat.

PETTICOAT
Cut 2 from red check.

CORNER
Stitch corners together
to dot before appliquéing.

Leave open.

INDEX

ABBREVIATIONS

KNITTING

ea	each
est	established
inc	increase
k	knit
p	purl
rep	repeat
rnd(s)	round(s)
sk	skip
st(s)	stitch(es)
tog	together

CROCHET

beg	begin(ning)	prev	previous
bk lp(s)	back loop(s)	rem	remain(s) (ing)
ch	chain(s)	rep	repeat(s)
dc	double crochet	rnd(s)	round(s)
dec	decrease(s) (d) (ing)	sc	single crochet
ea	each	sk	skip
est	established	sl st	slip stitch
foll	follow(s) (ing)	sp(s)	space(s)
ft lp(s)	front loop(s)	st(s)	stitch(es)
inc	increase(s) (d) (ing)	tog	together
lp(s)	loop(s)	yo	yarn over

CROSS-STITCH FABRIC AND DESIGN SIZE CONVERSION INFORMATION

To determine how many stitches can be taken per inch, measure 1" of your fabric and count the number of threads per inch. This is called a thread count. To determine the stitch count, count the number of stitches in the widest and longest portions of the graph. Divide the stitch count by the thread count to determine the finished design size, measured in inches. You should allow another 3" extra on each side of the design measurement to have enough fabric to work the design in a hoop and to give adequate space for finishing and framing.